WELSH
CASTLES
at War

C000053031

WELSH CASTLES
at War

JOHN NORRIS

TEMPUS

It is with great pleasure that I dedicate this book to my very good friends Chris Lay and Dave Biggins, in whose company I discovered many wonderful parts of Wales while on our walks. Thank you both.

First published 2004

Tempus Publishing Ltd
The Mill, Brimscombe Port
Stroud, Gloucestershire GL5 2QG
www.tempus-publishing.com

© John Norris, 2004

The right of John Norris to be identified as the Author
of this work has been asserted by him in accordance with the
Copyrights, Designs and Patents Act 1988.

All rights reserved. No part of this book may be reprinted
or reproduced or utilised in any form or by any electronic,
mechanical or other means, now known or hereafter invented,
including photocopying and recording, or in any information
storage or retrieval system, without the permission in writing
from the Publishers.

British Library Cataloguing in Publication Data.
A catalogue record for this book is available from the British Library.

ISBN 0 7524 2885 3

Typesetting and origination by Tempus Publishing.
Printed and bound in Great Britain.

CONTENTS

ACKNOWLEDGEMENTS

I would like to express my sincere gratitude to everybody who has made this work possible. Every member of staff, at the many different libraries, has always been most helpful, as have local residents at the many sites I had to visit during the course of compiling this work. I would like to particularly thank the site staff at the various castles administered by Cadw, from Caerphilly to Rhuddlan and across the breadth of this wonderful country of Wales. Their warmth, courtesy and hospitality were given freely and their knowledge of each site made my understanding that much more complete. I am also grateful, as ever, to my wife Elizabeth, who accompanied me on many field trips, often into remote parts of the countryside.

INTRODUCTION

The principality of Wales lies to the west of England and is bordered to the east by the English counties of Cheshire, Gloucestershire, Hereford, Shropshire and Worcestershire. The area covered by Wales, including the island of Anglesey, is some 20,768 sq. km (8,019 sq. miles), and into this expanse is concentrated the remains of hundreds of fortifications from many periods of history. The Welsh language is very old and one of several forms of dialect known as Celtic. For purposes of this work I have decided to use the English form of place names as they will be the most familiar terms to readers. This is unfortunate because, personally, I feel there is something very strong and evocative in the Welsh versions. Thus the reader will find Caerdydd is written as Cardiff and Caerfyrddin is written as Carmarthen.

It should be explained how some of the place names are pronounced. Many Welsh place names begin with a 'Ll' which has to be pronounced with the tongue at the back of the roof of the mouth to produce a guttural sound resembling 'hl'. This will be found in sites such as Llanstephan and Llandovery, the latter being written in Welsh as Llanymddyfri. The word 'Llan' itself means church and thus Llanstephan means the church of St Stephen. Place names beginning with the syllable 'Caer' indicate that they were fortified, because the term actually means 'fort'. Thus Caerphilly, Caergwrle and Caernarfon are indicative of the fact that they have at one time had a castle or been fortified in some manner. Likewise, when Cardiff and Carmarthen are written in their Welsh forms of Caerdydd and Caerfyrddin respectively, it would indicate the presence of castles. Finally, to clear up any questions regarding the consonants of double 'd' (dd), this is pronounced as 'th' as in 'they' and the double 'ff' is sounded as an 'f' but the single 'f', as in Dinefwr, is pronounced as a 'v'. These rules are applied to all proper names and will become clear as the history unfolds.

The country of Wales has a long and distinct history of military importance, even before the arrival of the Romans. Archaeological evidence shows there

1 Old map of Wales, showing outline of regions and boundaries

were more than 600 Iron Age hill forts by *c*.600 BC. With the arrival of the Romans certain important centres were expanded and the country was extensively mined for minerals such as iron, copper, gold and lead. The Romans even set about to deliberately 'Romanise' certain tribes, whom they could rely on to maintain order in the wild, inhospitable vastnesses of the hills. This was a tactic to be repeated many times by successive rulers, who could not afford to spare the manpower to keep rule in this remote region of their realm.*(1)*

When the Romans departed in the fifth century AD the whole country fell into a period, which today we know as the 'Dark Ages', when written history was very fragmented. The Welsh tribes, such as the Silures, were very warlike and raided into neighbouring territory. This led to the strengthening of hill forts and tribal areas being defined by natural or man-made landmarks such as earthworks and rivers.

Many castles in Wales have unfortunately been lost due to one reason or another, such as commercial development, and others played only a relatively small part in the military defence or conquest of the country. Some of these merit only a passing reference in keeping with the small part they played in the overall history of Wales. Others, although built as castles, can no longer in the real sense of the term be classified as such. Castell Coch, is one of these; although originally built in the fourteenth century, it was rebuilt in the nineteenth century as a stylised version of how the Victorians thought a medieval castle ought to look. Some have degenerated into nothing more than a pile of stones and rubble that bears no resemblance whatsoever to their former status. Some sites, such as Weobly castle, which although given the term 'castle' is really a fortified house, fall outside the remit of this work. So too, unfortunately, do the many hundreds of hill forts, which cannot be considered as true castles in the real sense of the term. Undoubtedly in their time they played a strategic part in the creation of the Welsh nation, when they were emblematic of a period many years before the great stone castles that the Normans brought with them.

During the medieval period there were some eighty castles built across the country at sites such as Cilgerran, Llawhaden, Llanstephan, Carew, Kidwelly and Caerphilly. Fortifications continued to feature predominantly and the trend lasted over the next several hundred years throughout the entire Middle Ages, with some 153 fortifications of various sizes and strengths erected on the borders between Wales and England. The thirteenth century saw a massive castle-building programme in Wales, the largest of its type anywhere in Europe, under the direction of Edward I. Each castle was only one day's march away from its nearest neighbouring site. These were very advanced in both design and concept, and the whole series was called his 'Iron ring', which was designed to control the Welsh. When he died the work was far from being completed and had brought the country to the verge of bankruptcy. When the Wars of the Roses ended in 1485, Henry Tudor, earl of Richmond, who was descended through Welsh ancestry, emerged as the victor and claimed the crown of England. It was ironic that the English, despite all the campaigns mounted against the Welsh (to subjugate the country), should end up with a Welsh king. The Tudor dynasty founded by Henry VII would go on to rule England for the next 116 years and establish the whole island of Britain as a dominating world force, not only in commerce but also military campaigns.

Many historians agree that for them and scholars alike, the reign of king Henry VIII very conveniently marks the true end of the Middle Ages. For over 400 years castles had been the symbol of the power which governed the land surrounding them. When Henry VII claimed the English throne, the very powerful weapon of gunpowder artillery was already changing the way in which wars were being fought and reshaping the designs of fortifications. When his son, Henry VIII, succeeded him, castles of the old period were being replaced by designs known as forts. These were purpose-built to incorporate artillery into their defensive measures and a world away from the great castle designs of the period of Edward I.

This work is about castles at war in Wales and the sieges they withstood. It concerns the coming of the castle proper to Wales in the wake of the Norman Conquest. It charts the rise and power of those castles. Obviously people do figure in this history, but it is their use of the castle and its function and power with which we are concerned.

1

THE COMING OF
THE NORMANS

In historical terms the area forming the border between England and Wales was always a very unsettled region. Bands of Welshmen frequently mounted cross-border raiding parties in order to steal cattle and other plunder. However, the regional differences went deeper on occasion and even spilled over into open conflict between rival tribes. But the Welsh natives and the country of Wales as we know it today only came into recognised existence by way of events following an act of treachery as they extended hospitality towards another tribe in the fifth century AD after the Romans had left Britain.

According to Chronicles written in the twelfth century by Geoffrey of Monmouth, when the Romans finally departed the country in the fifth century, after almost 500 years of occupation, the king of the Britons (whom he names as being either Gwrtheyrn or Vortigen) extended an offer to the Saxon leader Hengist and his brother, Horsa, suggesting they may sail to Britain and settle new lands with their followers. This was not a chance summoning, because Vortigen was actually married to Rowena, the daughter of Hengist. His intention was to utilise the experience of these warlike forces as mercenaries to protect him from attack by other tribes.

The offer was accepted and the Saxons journeyed to Britain with an initial force of some 600 men. They were followed later by another force of around 5,000 warriors, who settled in the area of Thanet. Here they were welcomed and made promises of great rewards in lands. As to only be expected from two vastly different cultures, it was an uneasy co-existence into which they settled. There were minor skirmishes between the two tribes, but despite the tensions daily life continued normally for about six years. Tensions finally came to a head one day when, during a conference between the tribal chiefs, the Saxons unexpectedly turned on the Britons and killed at least 300 of Voritgen's warriors, in an act which has been called the Brad Y Cyllyll Hirion, 'Treason of the Long Knives' (2). The name Vortigen is the most widely used title for

2   Representation showing the meeting between Vortigen (left) and Hengist the Saxon leader

the unfortunate tribal leader, but some historians now believe it may be a title equating to the term 'high chief'. But the fact that it is used as a proper name for a person and recorded as such in the history of the time is most telling. Geoffrey of Monmouth's work was entitled *Historia Regum Britanniae*, completed in *c*.1136, and pertains to be the history of Britain until the time of the death of Cadwaladr, the Welsh king, in AD 688. Only by cross-referencing with other early histories and the Brut can any of his facts be validated. For example, his history is supported by the earlier Chronicles of Gildas, a monk who wrote of the Saxon proceedings in AD 540, some ninety years after the events. Additionally there is the work of the Venerable Bede, a monk in the Northumbriam monastery of Jarrow, who, along with others of his day, substantiates this story, writing of how Hengist and Horsa came to Britain as mercenaries to defend the east coast and established the kingdom of Kent. Their arrival has been dated to around AD 450, and was followed later by other tribes, led by chieftains such as Aelle in AD 477 and Cerdic and Cynric in AD 495.

Under such pressure, the surviving Britons fled northwards and westwards to escape further slaughter by the Saxons and other invading tribes. Those fleeing west eventually found refuge in the remote hills and almost inaccessible valleys. The Saxons gave them the descriptive term of '*Wealas*' or '*Walas*', meaning either 'serfs' or 'foreigners'. From this very old root the present name of Wales has developed. For their part, the original Britons became known to outsiders as the Welsh, and were now, in effect, foreigners in their own lands. These displaced Britons in turn began to refer to themselves as '*Cymry*' which meant either 'comrades' or 'fellow-countrymen'. Persecuted as they were by the Saxons, and later the Angles, the dispossessed tribes became deeply suspicious and fiercely protective of the lands to which they had been forced. Although tribal in their ways, these displaced peoples were remarkably well organised and far from uncivilised, having established overseas trade with countries as diverse as France, Italy and Sicily. From the seventh century, an annual account of the important events surrounding their history was written as the 'Brut Y Tywysogion' ('Chronicles of the Princes'). These records, largely compiled and written by a succession of unknown scribes, tell of the fighting between the powerful families and the raids across the border, into what were now Saxon lands. The tribes in Wales at this time included the Cornovii, the Deceangli who settled Clwyd, Demetae in Pembroke, the Ordovices in Snowdonia and the Silures in the Glamorgan area. These were the Celtic tribes and in keeping with the old and traditional ways they created settlements centred on hill forts.

Among those tribes to settle in this manner was the fleeing Vortigen and his surviving followers. They settled at a site called Dinas Emrys, near Beddgelert, south-east of Caernarfon in Gwynedd. Not much in the way of hard evidence is known about this particular site, and what we do know has been pieced together using a cross between conjecture and circumspection. The remains which are visible at the site today are believed to date from around the thirteenth century and may have been built by a group of Welsh of unknown origin or allegiance. What we do know from these remains, however, is that the later troops to occupy the position must have realised how they could use the location to their own benefit and turn it into a strong and formidable defensive site. This is a feature which would occur many times in the later period of castle building in Wales, when sites not only dating from the time of Norman occupation but also Roman sites would be re-used by military engineers through to the reign of Edward I, after 1274.

The problem of cross-border raiding into England continued to be so serious that by the eighth century the Saxon king, Offa of Mercia, ordered that a huge ditch or 'dyke' be dug. The term 'dyke' was probably afforded to the excavation during its working, following an ancient tradition of so naming such earthworks. For example Wat's Dyke, which pre-dates Offa's Dyke, was a smaller earthwork dug around AD 600. What was different with Offa's Dyke was that it marked the western demarcation line of Mercia's territory, which he had won by the sword. It was ordered to run the entire length of the eastern border of Wales from the Dee estuary on the north coast, down through Herefordshire and Worcestershire, to terminate at the Severn estuary. The construction was meant to isolate the Welsh, and whilst it did not entirely eliminate the cross-border raiding, it did reduce it considerably. The theory has been proffered that the earthwork is not really a defensive work at all, but was created instead to present a visual and irrefutable boundary between Wales and England. It is known to have been excavated between AD 784 and AD 796, following a particularly fierce cross-border attack mounted by the Welsh in AD 784. However, the work can be viewed as being a cross between the two purposes because some sections of the so-called dyke have the shape of being a defensive work with steep sides.

In AD 822, the Mercian king Cenwulf invaded Wales, seizing areas of land, including Powys, and destroying the fortifications of Deganwy on the Conwy. This did nothing to subdue the Welsh, who retaliated by continuing to be an itinerant aggressor against whom the Saxons could never afford to relax their defences. If anything, they were obliged to maintain a series of vigilant patrols along the great dyke to guard against attacks, either provoked or otherwise. Today we still know this landmark as Offa's Dyke, which is still sufficiently defined enough to be marked on maps and to permit exploration.

The Welsh continued to be an unpredictable nation who would rise up against the Saxons with little or no provocation, despite the existence of Offa's protective earthwork. In the second half of the ninth century the Welsh were coalesced for the very first time under the leadership of Rhodri Mawr, who ruled much of central Wales. However this unity collapsed when Rhodri Mawr was killed in battle during an engagement against the Mercians in AD 878. He was followed by three other Welsh leaders who attempted to unify the country. His first successor was Hywel Dda, who laid down many laws to which the Welsh ascribed, before he died in AD 950. He in turn was succeeded by Maredudd ap Owain of Deheubarth, who died in AD 999. The last leader to take up the mantelet against the Saxons in this period was Gruffydd ap Llywelyn (sometimes written as Gruffudd ap Llywelyn), king of Gwynedd, and seen by some as the only native prince to rule the whole of Wales. He had been spurred into taking action because the Saxons were expanding beyond the western fringes of Offa's Dyke and he sought to put an end to this underhanded practice. This act of unity, which saw the Welsh raiding into Herefordshire, only served to incur the wrath of the Saxons in the form of Harold Godwinson, who was a harsh enemy. He invaded the country and overran Wales between 1062 and 1064, campaigning ruthlessly northwards to Snowdonia and destroying Gruffydd's palace at Rhuddlan by setting it on fire. With the war going badly against them, the first signs of disunity were beginning to show among the Welsh and some of Gruffydd's troops and leaders deserted him.

Exactly how Gruffydd met his demise is not entirely clear. Some records state that he was killed in a Saxon ambush, while other accounts state he was killed by his own men who had revolted against his leadership and who decapitated him. They presented his head to Harold, who then demanded that Gruffydd's two half-brothers swear allegiance to the Saxon regency in England. With Gruffydd now dead and subservient local leaders in place, it appeared that for the first time in centuries the Welsh border would be settled. It is quite possible that Gruffydd's demise may be a combination of both versions: being led into a trap by his own troops who were no longer loyal, who then turned on him and killed him. What is certain is the fact that it would be almost another 200 years before the Welsh would find themselves once more truly united against the Normans and Saxons as the common enemy.

In January 1066, Harold Godwinson was elected king by the Witan, when Edward the Confessor died. But as king, Harold II's realm was, in reality, under threat from all quarters. On 25 September that year Harold engaged a massive Viking army, which had landed in Northumbria from a fleet of 300 ships, at the battle of Stamford Bridge. So complete was his victory that chronicles tell how the defeated Vikings required only twenty-four ships to take away the survivors. Three weeks later, on 14 October, and after a 250-mile forced march, Harold's army had to face a French invasion force of considerable size, led by Duke William of Normandy, at the battle of Hastings or Senlac Hill, in East Sussex. The exact size of the French army is not known, but historians agree that it was not less than 9,000 men. Harold's army was about 10,000 men and during the fierce battle which developed he was killed, leading to the collapse of the Saxon army which broke ranks and fled the battlefield. The death of this oppressor of the Welsh was triumphantly recorded in the 'Brut Y Tywysogion', which notes the fact as:

> A certain man called William the Bastard, leader of the Normans, and with him a mighty host, came against him [Harold Godwinson]; and after a mighty battle and a slaughter of the Saxons, he despoiled him of his kingdom and of his life, and he defended for himself the kingdom of the Saxons with victorious hand and a mighty noble host.

However, had they known, the rejoicing would be short-lived, because as the Welsh would soon discover, the French Norman knights would prove to be equally strict overlords.

As with the rest of Britain, Wales had suffered greatly from Viking raids during the tenth century, and these experiences had strengthened the fighting prowess of the warrior caste within the tribes. Throughout the tenth century the Vikings had attacked mainly coastal regions of Wales and taken large numbers of prisoners, which they then traded as slaves with other communities. The Vikings, for some inexplicable reason, did not seek to exploit the weak tribal opposition facing them in Wales, and did not even try to establish a permanent settlement. One of the suggested reasons why the Vikings did not attempt to conquer Wales is perhaps that the country lacked viable economic resources. This is an arguable point, because the country had mineral wealth such as gold and copper, both of which were highly prized metals. Over the intervening period of 500 years, since the time when the Romans had left, those dispossessed tribes now referred to as the Welsh had learned many lessons of warfare and adapted a unique set of battle tactics to suit the harsh terrain in which they had settled. The tribal leaders at the time of the Norman Conquest were in effect local warlords, the allegiance to whom was owed only by one's immediate retinue and villagers. The country, at this time was divided into several areas: Brycheiniog, Deheubarth, Dyfed, Gwent, Gwynedd, Morgannwg and Powys. These were known as Gwledydd or small kingdoms, which were divided into territories, known as *cantrefi* (hundreds). These in turn were divided into smaller areas known as either *cymydau* or commotes, which were ruled by powerful local families who held court or Llys in those regions they controlled.

Messengers brought news of the Norman French victory at the battle of Hastings to Wales, where most ruling factions realised that it would only be a question of time before the victorious French had consolidated their newly won territories sufficiently to allow them to move westwards. Once this happened they knew the Normans would want to extend their rule across the whole country. As the first Norman king of Britain, William not only had to settle his newly conquered lands, he also had to contend with rebellion from certain of his nobles, continued Danish attacks on the coast and entreaties from France. It was because of these immediate problems, as much as anything else, that Wales was prevented from feeling the full impact of the Norman regime for some time. Along with its remoteness the country would, for the time being at least, be spared the imposing of new and strict laws governing the conquered lands. Indeed, King William gave the appearance of not being overly interested in the investment of Wales, being more content in the knowledge that the peace was kept instead.

This assumption is borne out by the fact that King William sought to reach a compromise with the Welsh through the use of intermediaries *(3)*. During negotiations his emissaries sought on their king's behalf to bring about some semblance of order for the first time through correspondence and entreaties, negotiating with the likes of Rhys ap Tewdwr, ruler of Deheubarth and a prominent figure among leading Welsh families. Despite being isolated from courtly politics, Rhys ap Tewdwr was wise enough to realise the advantage there would be in having a pact with King William, which protected him from direct action by the Norman earls, but he was far from being a passive or submissive leader. Believing Rhys ap Tewdwr to be a trusted Norman vassal who would keep the peace, he was left to his own devices. But with a figure-head as shrewd as Rhys this was to prove an unwise decision. The Normans

3 King William I, first Norman king of England, who acceded to the throne in 1066

were not to immediately discover their mistaken trust in him. He knew how to bide his time and lull them into a false sense of security. He finally took up arms and mounted a campaign against his Norman masters in 1073 and 1074, which forced them to withdraw. But he was safe in the knowledge that with his due tribute paid to King William no Norman lord would dare to challenge Rhys, for he was a king's man. He had great prowess and would continue to exploit his position and be a source of great annoyance until his death in 1093.

There was no overall kingship in Wales, being instead a series of individual kingships covering tribal areas. In historical terms, consolidation and unity were not things that came readily to the various tribes. Indeed, it was not until the arrival of the first Norman representatives, around 1067, when some form of cohesion began to take place, by which time it was too late for the Welsh to take any action. The Normans were to prove themselves determined to remain and control the country as the true rulers, which would include the use of force when necessary.

The Normans, realising the magnitude of the task before them, were content to just watch over the border area from seats of power in the form of three powerful earldoms. These were 'Fat' Hugh, 'The Wolf' of Avranches as earl of Chester; William fitz Osbern (sometimes written as Osborn) as earl of

Hereford; and Roger of Montgomery as earl of Shrewsbury. But these Norman earls were not satisfied in simply maintaining the status quo along the border, and on occasion they sallied forth into Wales to take advantage of the country torn apart internally since the death of Gruffudd ap Llywelyn in 1063.

The initial penetrations made into Wales by these three men were in effect small invasions, and almost certainly conducted without the king's knowledge or permission. But the fact that all three were held in high regard by the king meant they could act with almost total impunity, and had the king known it is unlikely he would have sanctioned them. All three were favourites of the king and very ambitious knights, but of them it was probably fitz Osbern who had the strongest character. He certainly established the most power and between 1067 and 1071 is credited with the building of Chepstow castle, the first stone fortification in Wales. He also went on to found his lordship in Strigoil, southern Gwent.

By 1081 these border-guarding earls were acting virtually independently and in an autocratic manner, with King William apparently being completely unconcerned or unaware of their actions. In 1088, Fat Hugh had pushed into north Wales along the coast and had established a castle at Aberlleinog on the east coast of Anglesey, near Penmon. He had also built castles at Bangor and Caernarfon. In fact, such was the pressure he put on North Wales that civil war erupted in Gwynedd *(4)*.

4 Opposite left Recreated Norman knight, showing the mail armour and 'kite-shaped' shield and use of cavalry in battle

5 Opposite right Recreated mounted Norman knights wearing mail armour and armed with swords and carrying 'kite-shaped' shields

6 Right Recreated Saxon warrior armed with an axe and wearing conical helmet. This style of equipment would have also been used in Wales at the time of the Norman invasion

The Normans were beginning to build their first permanent castles in Wales in the form known as motte and bailey, and it would be through the presence of these fortifications which the Normans would establish themselves across the country *(5)*. The likes of such castles had never been seen before, and a chronicler recorded in the 'Brut Y Tywysogion' that: 'The French overran Dyfed and Ceredigion… And made castles in them and fortified them.' It was blatantly clear to all concerned that the Normans were very positively staying put in Wales and were consolidating their most recent acquisitions. These motte-and-bailey castles were very basic, at first being little more than earth and timber which only later would develop into stone castles. The section known as the motte was usually a natural feature such as a hill, or a small mound which the Normans shaped to suit their needs by adding layers of earth to increase the height. On top of this was constructed a wooden palisade, in which the garrison could live and store provisions, and the whole site surrounded by a stone or timber wall known as the bailey.

The first Normans to arrive in Wales appear to have contented themselves with taking up locations along the borders and consolidating their positions. In fact, it was not until 1072 that the Brut makes the first positive mention of the Norman presence in Wales, when entries record how Marredudd ab Owain of Deheubarth was killed by Caradog ap Gruffydd of Gwent, who was supported by the 'French', as it is put *(6)*. This in itself is not conclusive proof of evidence that the Normans were beginning to make inroads into Wales, but rather points to the fact that they were involving themselves with skirmishes and localised fighting between regional rulers. This type of action can be viewed more like interference and is not indicative of direct political support. On this occasion the move was certainly not unusual, because the Normans were known to provide aid to a local ruler and shows how they were shrewd enough to give their support to whoever they thought could aid them in their Conquest and settle the lands.

Three years before the Norman Conquest, the ruler of Gwynedd had been Bleddyn ap Cynfyn. In the year 1063 he had sworn fealty to King Edward on an oath which was carried on into the reign of William, the great-nephew of the late King Edward, after his victory at Hastings on 14 October 1066. As a result of this Bleddyn was a protégé of the king and during the reign of King William could not be challenged by any Norman. However, that did not protect from his own countrymen and he was attacked and killed by Rhys ab Owain of Deheubarth in 1075. His place was taken by Rhys's cousin, Trahaearn ap Caradog, who ruled Arwystli a small kingdom in mid-Wales. This marked the beginning of a period of serious inter-rivalry fighting between Welsh rulers. With no recognised native ruler, certainly none recognised by William of England, the country erupted into disorder. This situation was not unusual, and it has been ascertained through chronicles that between the years AD 949 and 1066 some thirty-five Welsh rulers died at the hands of other Welshmen in such arguments.

Into this troubled state of affairs came various figures, such as Gruffydd ap Cynan ab Iago, returning from exile in Dublin. He was the son of Cynan ap Iago whose father had been king of Gwynedd before being overthrown by Gruffydd ap Llywelyn who had been killed in 1063, and he arrived to challenge Trahaearn ap Caradog for his rightful inheritance of Gwynedd. In his band of warriors he had a number of Viking mercenaries, but they were considered to be unreliable. To back him in his claim Gruffydd ap Cynan also had the aid of some sixty Norman knights. Despite being well supported he was defeated at the battle of Bron Yr Erw and his campaign collapsed forcing him to return to Ireland, leaving Trehaearn still ruling Gwynedd. However, he in turn was under pressure from Norman troops, raiding down to the Llyn Peninsular from Chester, with the support of Welshmen from Powys, under the command of Gwrgan ap Seisyll.

In 1081 Trahaearn was challenged again, but this time by Rhys ap Tewdwr, the claimant to Deheubarth. He too was supported by Viking mercenaries and with this force he met Trahaearn in battle at the site of Mynydd Carn, generally believed to be located somewhere in south-west Wales. His army was more successful and they defeated and killed Trahaearn in battle. Caradog ap Gruffydd, who had taken Deheubarth, was forced to flee from the field of battle. Rhys ap Tewdwr was now instated as the ruler of his conquered territories. Gruffydd ap Cynan of Gwynedd had been taken prisoner by the Normans and imprisoned in Chester castle. This now left Gwynedd without a ruler and so Robert of Rhuddlan, a relative of the earl of Chester, seized on the opportunity to take power. He would remain in control for twelve years until killed in 1093 when his castle at Degannwy on the Conwy estuary was attacked by a force led by Gruffydd ap Cynan, who had by then escaped from Chester. Although termed a castle, it is possible that Robert of Rhuddlan's stronghold at Degannwy may have been either a motte-and-bailey type structure or a modified hill fort. In which case, it would have fallen relatively easily to a force which could have destroyed it by setting fire to the wooden structures.

The year of 1081 was to be a decisive turning point for Wales and the Welsh. Events took a turn as Rhys ap Tewdwr, still flushed with his victory at Mynydd Carn, entered the power struggle with renewed vigour. The Normans were alerted to the success and popularity of this Welsh prince, who is recorded in Domesday Book and given the title '*Riset*'. This book was a record of King William's realm and in it is recorded how a particular king in south Wales, understood to be Rhys ap Tewdwr, paid £40 tribute per annum for his tenure of Deheubarth and became William's vassal. This freed him from Norman intervention, and Rhys could now use his newly won trust to conspire his next move against the Normans.

In the same year King William, a deeply religious man, undertook a great pilgrimage to St Davids. Some believed it was his great piety which caused him to journey to the holy site where Bishop Bernard had been killed by Viking raiders only the year before in 1080. Others believed that William embarked on his journey with an ulterior motive: to see the situation in Wales for himself. His entourage, which included a large military bodyguard, was no doubt intended to send out the message to Rhys ap Tewdwr and other Welsh princes, that he would no longer tolerate Viking mercenaries being brought to the country to fight Normans. The truth is probably somewhere between the two reasons, with William using his journey as a propaganda ploy. One thing is certain, with such a display of strength, he could move through the country with impunity and the force had little to fear in the way of an organised attack. In other words, the whole column was really a show of military strength to demonstrate to the Welsh just how well organised the Normans were. The military situation was developing into one of such uniqueness, with either side wishing to rid the country of the other, that they were prepared to use one another, or indeed any means necessary, to achieve their aims. As a direct consequence of his visit in 1081, it is believed that it was King William himself who ordered the building of Cardiff castle *(7)*.

As it transpired, the building at Cardiff would not be started until 1091, four years after the death of William I, by Robert fitz Hamo (sometimes written as Robert Fitzhamon) who held power in Bristol and Gloucester. As with other

7   Cardiff castle, built on the orders of William I. It evolved from a wooden motte-and-bailey style into the stone-walled 'shell keep' as seen here

castles at this time, Cardiff was originally a motte-and-bailey type design with a surrounding moat *(8)*. The castle was well placed and intended to cover the approaches of the important Taff estuary waterway. In time Cardiff castle would be developed into a formidable fortress and used as the seat of lordship by the native Welsh rulers of the uplands. The site had formerly been used by the Romans and the obvious importance of the location for the latest Norman fort was not lost on the military planners. It was in this year that work also commenced on Pembroke castle, another site previously used by the Romans. Again, at first, this was a motte-and-bailey design built by Arnulf of Montgomery, but would later come to be developed and command the waterway leading to Milford Haven.

The motte-and-bailey design of fortification was the virtual hallmark of the early Norman defensive system. It was a style that they brought to Britain with them and was characterised by the two elements within the design. The first part of the defensive structure was the motte, which was simply a mound where the keep, or donjon, fortification could be erected for housing the troops and their stores. The motte could be incorporated into the structure of the fortification in a number of ways. For example, it could be a natural feature which

8 The stone keep of Cardiff castle, which can be traced back to 1081 when King William I ordered the castle to be built

the Normans would alter to suit their needs by shaping it to fit their specific requirements through a force of labourers. In this instance it would be altered to give a conical shape with only one direct route of access to the summit on which the donjon would be built. The name donjon is believed to be a corruption of an ancient term, possibly Latin, which originally meant dominating point. Another method was to create a suitable motte by digging a circular ditch and use the resulting spoil to develop the feature into the desired conical shape and keep adding to it in order to increase the height. The ditch would then be incorporated into the defensive network of the site. This method was labour intensive and could take months to complete the work. Mottes could vary in height from only 16ft to as much as 65ft. Not only did the summit of a motte serve as a platform for the keep, it also served to provide the garrison lookout with an unrestricted view over the surrounding topography.

The bailey was the walled area at the foot of the motte and totally surrounded it, enclosing any buildings directly associated with the development of the site. The gateway into the compound was located here and once inside allowed access to the keep at the top of the motte. The ditch which ran around the circumference of the site, usually outside the bailey walls, would have presented any would-be attacker with another obstacle to overcome. This feature was usually dry and sometimes filled with thorn bushes, such as brambles or blackthorn, in the manner of very early barbed wire. Later, some sites would develop a system which allowed the flooding of the surrounding ditch, in order to present an attacker with a water obstacle, and later still this would become commonly referred to as a moat.

Motte-and-bailey sites were the first defensive measures constructed after the Norman Conquest, because they were relatively inexpensive, easily raised and could be built on site using materials available locally. Some historians believe that the more simple motte-and-bailey sites may have taken as little as two weeks to complete. These would have been very basic and quite small. The more complicated and larger sites would have taken longer to complete, perhaps even months. However, it was these larger sites which would eventually be developed into the permanent stone castles to which further additions were made during later periods. Such locations would be altered to incorporate the latest emerging fortification styles over the years. These more complex motte-and-bailey designs would have used double walls and even double ditches to surround the bailey. The sites were widely dispersed in order to control as much of the region as possible and that made them vulnerable. The Welsh at first lacked the means to directly attack these strategic positions and simply bypassed them and cut them off to prevent reinforcements and supplies getting through. Denied of support, the garrison would be forced out and would withdraw into areas more strongly held by Normans. The Welsh were able to use the terrain to their own advantage and could withdraw into the hills when the situation went against them.

One of the earliest and strongest of the motte-and-bailey sites raised by the Normans in Wales was that built by Roger of Montgomery, the first Norman earl of Shrewsbury, around 1071. Located on the western edge or Welsh side of Offa's Dyke, the site, known as Hen Domen, offered the garrison a commanding view over the River Severn. Archaeological excavations have revealed that the site was very important despite the fact that it was relatively small. Hen Domen was well protected and had very strong defences, incorporating the double-ditch system to surround the oval-shaped bailey. The motte was located at the western side of the bailey, which also had two ramparts constructed from the earth dug from the ditches. The walls were wooden, as were the other first types of motte-and-bailey fortifications at this time. It is very obvious that a series of fortifications, such as Hen Domen, were built as a form of smokescreen as the Normans advanced westwards. This is evident from the fact that another of Roger of Montgomery's motte-and-bailey sites was built about 1 mile south-east of the present Cardigan castle. Here too, excavations have proved the existence of the castle, but little remains of it today

Earl Roger of Montgomery was a favourite of King William, but unlike his fellow earl and comrade in arms, William fitz Osbern, he was not so

9 King William II who succeeded as king on the death of his father, William I

magnanimous in his rule. From his castle at Hen Domen he raided into several areas, including Cynllaith, Edeirion, Nanheudwy, Ial, Ceri, Cydewain and Arwystli. Montgomery raised castles elsewhere, most notably Oswestry, from where he conducted raids into northern parts of Wales. However, his most impressive by far was the construction of Pembroke castle, which was started *c.*1090–1091. Some historians date the beginning of Pembroke castle to 1093, but the truth of the matter is that it was established by Roger of Montgomery and is built on a spit of land which juts out from the bank of the River Pembroke to form a natural water obstacle on three sides of the site. The castle was built in the motte-and-bailey style with a wooden palisade. The confusion surrounding the date of building on the site may stem from the fact that Roger's younger son, Arnulf, arrived there in 1093 and was created custodian of the castle. When Arnulf was called to England he handed over custody of the castle to Gerald of Windsor, leaving a small garrison to guard the site.

In 1094 a major uprising of the Welsh took place, with forces known to have been directed against the area controlled by the castle's garrison. It has been argued that this may have been in belated support of the uprising instigated by Rhys ap Tewdwer. At first, one is inclined to believe that it was a completely localised uprising in response to the building of the castle and totally unrelated to the cause championed by Rhys ap Tewdwer, who had, in any case, been killed the year before. We do know that, when the Normans invaded the area of Dyfed in 1093, the local Welsh were incensed, and this, coupled with the death of Rhys ap Tewdwer, led to the uprising. The monarch at the time was King William II, the son of Willam the Conqueror, and he was in the seventh year of his reign *(9)*. When the Welsh uprising started he was in France, but had he been in England it is unlikely that he could have done much to personally resolve the situation.

According to the Brut the Welsh plundered around Pembroke and 'returned home with vast spoil'. The uprising now spread into north and south Wales as the country erupted into full-scale war against the Normans. Pembroke castle was besieged, which, given the size of the site and the resources available to the Welsh, would have meant investing the location with a significant encampment. This is borne out by the fact that the Welsh force was led by Cadwgan ap Beddyn ap Cynfyn, king of Powys. It was a very serious situation for the defending garrison and Gerald of Windsor, whose reputation as an effective commander was at stake. Siege tactics used by the Welsh against castles at this time were restricted to burning the wooden structures or starving out the garrison. There was nothing subtle about either tactic, but given the right circumstances they could produce the desired result – the surrender of the castle. It should be remembered, however, that these tactics were widely employed, even by the Normans themselves, simply because they knew of no other way to attack a defensive site at the time. Tactics such as scaling the timber palisades using ladders or attacking the gates with a battering ram to smash a way in were not as yet developed.

At this period any force laying siege to a castle could only rely on the two tried and proven methods of attempting to induce the garrison to surrender. Fire was dreaded and a constant vigilance had to be maintained against it breaking out, either through accident or being deliberately started by an attacking enemy. When a castle was isolated from the possibility of a relief force supplies of food, water and arrows were restricted. The longer a siege lasted the greater the chance of capturing the castle. There was no way of knowing how long a siege would have to last to achieve this and whether the garrison was strong enough to hold out for a prolonged period, the defenders may also begin to suffer due to poor sanitation and dwindling morale in a stagnating encampment. As time wore on other means of attacking castles came into use, including mining to dig under the walls and launching heavy stones from catapults to pound the defences. However in the late eleventh century these refinements were still some way off and siege warfare was really a question of attrition. The Welsh realised their limitations and knew that if they could prevent a relief force from reaching a castle under siege, there was every chance they could win the situation. It was up to the Normans to prevent this from happening, and as is to be expected there were mixed results in such circumstances.

The Welsh force besieging Pembroke castle in 1094 were in a strong position, whilst the defenders of the castle were running short of supplies and morale was waning. As the siege wore on, conditions inside the castle deteriorated to such a low point that fifteen of the Norman knights in the garrison deserted their posts under cover of darkness. Their fate is not known for certain, but one can surmise they would not have lived long if they were captured by the Welsh. As deserters they would have had no ransom value to the Normans, who would have punished them, in any case, had they returned. In an effort to reverse what was a tremendous shock to morale, Gerald of Windsor elected fifteen men from the garrison as knights and transferred the estates of the errant knights to those he had created.

Gerald then produced a strategic defensive plan based on the use of tact and guile, through which he hoped to bluff his way out of the situation. Although stocks of food were dwindling he ordered that four pigs be butchered in view of the besiegers and the carcases thrown over the walls. Through this act he hoped to show his contempt for the way in which the Welsh were trying to starve him into submission. The action of throwing away food stocks was intended to prove the garrison had sufficient supplies to allow such a waste and that they were not starving. He reinforced this by writing a letter to Arnulf, in which he claimed he could withstand the siege for another four months before requiring more troops and provisions. This document was made more valid by the fact that it bore Gerald's personal seal. It was arranged that the letter should fall into the hands of the besiegers. Shortly after these incidents the Welsh broke camp and departed, leaving the castle unassaulted. Gerald had gambled a great deal and his survival depended on a successful outcome. He later claimed the Welsh were completely taken in by his bluff. In view of the fact the defenders did not show signs of weakening, one might think the Welsh were being fooled by the ruse. Cadwgan may have decided that the castle's defences and garrison were too strong and he did not want to waste his forces in a protracted siege which could, in turn, leave them open to disease as was often the case in besiegers' camps. Pembroke castle had been one of the key fortresses in Wales and with the failure of the Welsh to seize it, the uprising of 1094 collapsed.

One of the earliest attempts at besieging a Norman castle by the Welsh had failed, but it was not the only failure during the uprising of 1094. The site of Rhydygors (sometimes written as Rhyd-Y-Gors), today known as Carmarthen, was also invested. In 1093 the Norman knight of William fitz Baldwin had established a motte–and–bailey castle at the site when he sailed up the River Tywi during the Norman invasion of Dyfed. The original site is unfortunately now completely lost and its location unknown. The remains of the stone castle one sees in Carmarthen today is a different location to the original Rhydygors and was raised on the foundations of a later motte–and–bailey castle.

The sieges at Pembroke and Rhydygors may have been failures but at other sites the Welsh fared much better in reducing the Norman castles by resorting to the two methods available, which were burning and starvation. For example, the motte-and-bailey site at Cardigan, established by earl Roger of

Montgomery, was so completely destroyed that the site was abandoned. In fact, so successful were the Welsh that they managed to push the Normans back from Ceredigion, after the siege of Cardigan, and even re-conquered the area of Dyfed. This left only those two major sites where the Welsh failed to be held by the Normans. In 1096 the site at Rhydygors was abandoned following the death of William fitz Baldwin, at which time the Welsh moved in and destroyed it. It is now believed that the original fortification on the site may never have been completed. Rhydygors (Carmarthen) would not be re-fortified until 1105, when Richard fitz Baldwin established another castle to dominate the River Towy. At the time of the abandonment of Rhydygors, only Pembroke was left as a Norman outpost in area covered by an over-stretched occupying power.

The historian P.R. Davis in his book *Castles of the Welsh Princes* states:

> The castle was the key to the Normans' success in maintaining a military presence in an invaded territory. Earth and timber fortifications could be set up in a short time to consolidate newly conquered lands, to guard strategic areas and to act as bases for further operations.

He was absolutely correct; however, such defences were not as enduring as stone, and the early wooden stockade walls had to be replaced when they rotted due to the natural process of weathering. Another risk was that being wooden they were vulnerable to burning. A garrison would have been constantly on the lookout for uncontrolled fires and engaged in repairing the walls. The living quarters would also have been built using timber and therefore vulnerable when attackers employed fire as a 'weapon'.

The early motte-and-bailey castles could be built by a labour force under the direction of a military engineer versed in the ways of constructing such fortifications. It has been suggested that the smaller, more simple motte-and-bailey sites may have taken as little as two weeks to build. Depending on the size of the work force this is quite possible. Material would have been available locally and once the site was secure, the garrison could have taken up residence. After that it would be expanded and further buildings erected from a safe working base.

Whilst the motte-and-bailey design of castle was good in its day, it was obvious to many that the standard design could be improved and expanded, rather than just modified to use stone instead of timber. However, it took a transitional period of change over almost 200 years for the traditional motte-and-bailey design to evolve into the formidable castles of the Middle Ages. In 1095 a number of European monarchs and nobles, including William Rufus, became involved in supporting the first of a series of holy wars, known as Crusades. Kings either led their troops in person, or in the case of William Rufus, were content to allow Norman nobles to campaign in these distant wars. The object of the Crusades was to protect the revered 'Holy Places' of Christendom from being taken over by the perceived threat of Muslim expansionism. The main problem surrounding these wars in a country so far from England was the severe strain they placed on resources in manpower, money and equipment. The armies had to be transported at great cost, all of which meant that military forces at home had to be denied material and finances. For almost 200 years and over some eight separate campaigns these holy wars were fought. One consequence of these wars was the fact that returning knights, military observers and chroniclers brought back with them many ideas for improving battlefield tactics and new weaponry. Another of the new ideas the knights brought back was for the design of a new style of castle layout. These new castles, known as 'walls within walls' were influenced by the castles they had seen in the Middle East.

The most important lesson they learned from the Crusades was the fact that the new castles had to be built entirely from stone, from the foundation upwards. This was for a number of obvious reasons, not the least being that such building material would allow larger, more powerful castles to be erected. Stone is also more enduring, and unlike wood, is not vulnerable to burning and does not rot. The knights and military engineers also learned about special engines which could be used in sieges to hurl large stone projectiles to batter the walls of castles. This new influence meant that purpose-built castles were constructed and the original motte-and-bailey styles could be upgraded more efficiently. One of the first castles to benefit from this upgrading was the Norman castle of Bronllys, which dated from the 1060s. This site typifies how it was possible to modify an original motte-and-bailey style, as built on the banks of the River Lynfi between Brecon and Hay. The donjon on the motte of this site was rebuilt in stone over the years, so that by around 1176 Bronllys had been transformed into a castle with an impressive round tower of three storeys. Rebuilt in stone, it now stood some 80ft high and was of such a substantial design that two passages were incorporated within the thickness of the walls. This meant that the defenders could move from one part of the tower's defences to another without being exposed to the attackers. Bronllys was used by William Rufus as a base of operations during his two campaigns into Wales in 1095 and again in 1097, almost certainly before it was remodelled. Later tenants included the Bohuns and eventually the Stafford family during the reign of Henry VII, after 1485. The defence of the site benefited from the new style which would have been most impressive at the height of its power.

Another motte-and-bailey design to be transformed into a stone castle as a result of influences brought back from the Crusades was the site at Hay-on-Wye. The word 'Hay' is believed to be a corruption of the French word '*haie*' to mean enclose with a hurdle, and would appear to be a reference to the bailey area at the base of the original mound which formed the motte. The site originated in the 1060s and was one of the first to be erected in the area when the Normans arrived. During the twelfth century Hay-on-Wye was remodelled and built in stone. Whilst this made it a structure of more stout design, capable of withstanding an attack more effectually, it did draw attention to itself by virtue of the fact that it was a symbol of Norman control and a real stronghold. It was to be political manoeuvrings rather than direct military action which brought about the fall of the garrison. The castle at Hay-on-Wye was still considered worthy of the attention of forces led by Owain Glyn Dwr after 1400 and the town and castle were destroyed. It never regained any military importance and today is in private possession.

Many other motte-and-bailey castles were to be remodelled over the years and converted into stone structures. Two such sites were both called Newport; one in Gwent and the other in Dyfed. The Newport castle in Gwent, standing on the River Usk, originally a Norman castle, was rebuilt so that by the fourteenth century it incorporated three towers directly into the design of the curtain walls. This was a feature not possible with wooden structures and showed the way forward in improved defences. It was remodelled but was eventually sacked by the forces of Owain Glyn Dwr after 1401. The castle of Newport in Dyfed was originally built in the eleventh century by Sir William fitz Martin after the motte-and-bailey castle at Nevern had been captured by the Welsh. The castle was moved and developed over the years so that by the twelfth century it had been rebuilt in stone and used the estuary of the River Nyfer as part of its defences. In fact, it seems that wherever possible castles throughout Wales used natural water obstacles, especially rivers, as part of their defences. This not only prevented attackers from approaching the base of the castle walls to attack them, the waterway also meant the walls could not be undermined. Waterways also ensured that castles could be resupplied by boats sailing right up to the castle itself. At Newport castle in Gwent a special water gate was built between two angle towers to allow boats to sail into a completely enclosed dock area, 35ft long and 20ft wide. From here they could unload their cargo in total safety within the confines of the castle's defences.

These early defensive constructions were not powerful enough in their own right, and they simply served to act as a base from which the Normans would order out light forces to control the local tribes. These patrols could move from one such outpost to another and attempt to subdue the country. Castles in the Norman sense of the term were the private fortresses of the king or nobles and were the product of the feudal system, which grew strong as a result of the weakness of other systems and was based on the services of vassals directly to the king, who, by way of acknowledging their loyalty, were awarded grants of land. Castles had been used in this manner in European military societies since the ninth century, but their likes had never before been witnessed in England and certainly not in Wales. Under the Normans, the castle not only served as a base from which the garrison could operate, it was also an administrative

10   The outer, or curtain, walls of Chepstow castle, the first stone castle to be built in Wales

centre and a location from which further inroads could be made to strength-ening the occupation of the country. This was certainly to be the case in both Chepstow and Montgomery.

Chepstow castle was to be the lasting legacy left by fitz Osbern, being the first of its kind to be built from stone almost from the time it was laid out *(10)*. He had also founded the lordship of Strigoil in southern Gwent. This was a very brave move on his part for the men of Gwent were described as being 'fierce-fighting... marked by a peculiarly unscrupulous ruthlessness.' It was already general knowledge that the Welsh hated any form of restraint and were, 'devoted to an irregular warfare of surprises and even treachery.' This left fitz Osbern open to attack at any time. His castle at Chepstow was started in 1067 and work continued until 1071, by which time he was on the king's service in Flanders and probably even killed during the course of that service.

William fitz Osbern was able to garrison his castle at Chepstow by offering rich rewards to attract knights into his service *(11)*. This was something few knights would want to miss and many moved into the area he controlled on the Welsh border. At the same time there were many Welsh settling in the same area, and no doubt not wishing to create any enmity towards himself, fitz Osbern decided it was more prudent to leave them alone. Untroubled as they were, these Welsh settlers enjoyed better privileges than many of their fellow

11 The gatehouse of Chepstow castle, showing the inherent strength of the structure

countrymen, with the direct endorsement of the earl himself. However, this peaceful co-existence did not last for long. In 1070 fitz Osbern as one of King William's most trusted nobles was sent back to France. He was known as 'the bravest of all the Normans.' It was probably his reliability and close association with the king which led William to charge fitz Osbern with returning to France to put his affairs in order. He was killed in Flanders whilst on service for the king. Before he left for France, he had placed his second son in charge of his affairs, and when he was killed in 1071 his son assumed all his possessions. Not being as wise as his father he rebelled against King William, and he and his forces were attacked, after which he was imprisoned for his actions. The lands and estates of the family were confiscated and were to remain in abeyance until 1125. This insurrection led to a weakening of the Norman presence on the border and would ultimately have severe consequences.

Chepstow castle is unique for a number of reasons, not the least because it was one of the first castles to be built with the specific intention of bringing about Norman control of Wales. The castle was built on a site at the bottom of a hill by the River Wye, and not on the summit as was the usual method which permitted the garrison a complete and unrestricted view in all directions. Also, it was built without a keep in the proper sense of the word. The decision to build the castle where it stands was probably regulated by geological topography which prevented it from being raised as the more traditional motte-and-bailey style. This leads one to question: why build it there if that were the case? The answer is really very simple: because it stands on the River Wye, which would not only have supplied fresh water, but which could also be incorporated into its defences. As for the lack of a keep, this could be explained by the fact the fitz Osbern may simply have wished to keep the design simple in order to speed up the building work or keep costs down.

The castle is bounded to one side by a ridge which runs east–west whilst to the north a rock face lies above the River Wye and to the south is a steep ravine. The castle was built on the narrowest part of the ridge. It was divided into two baileys, the middle or east and the upper or west, with connecting walls. The stone hall has been called a keep by some historians, probably because it was remodelled by successive occupants to show some development into a keep. Chepstow was extremely strong, having walls up to 9ft thick, and would serve as the benchmark by which other Norman castles, not only in Wales but across England, would follow by example. Indeed, it may have been this obvious strength which precluded it from being attacked or besieged until the seventeenth century and the English Civil War.

However, the rugged and undulating terrain of the Welsh country was not conducive to Norman cavalry tactics, which greatly hampered their progress and slowed down their process of occupation. The Normans quickly realised this and adopted the tried-and-tested method of winning over sympathetic tribal leaders and their followers, through a range of inducements which included the granting of lands in the newly occupied territory and even simply providing adequate supplies of food. It was these co-operative Welsh troops raised in the area known as the Marches, which would be fundamental to the overall success in bringing the country under some sort of control. Gradually the Welsh were being worn down through military action or won over to the Norman ways, in a manner very similar to how the Romans had operated many centuries before.

The Normans in that respect were very astute and realised the importance of building their castles in the most strategic positions possible. This is exactly what happened in the case of Cardiff, which was built on a site that had previously been used by the Romans as a fort and base of operations. In time, as the original motte-and-bailey designs developed into the stone buildings, the Welsh lost the capability to attack these castles. The Normans would have realised this and continued the transition to building in stone.

Building castles from stone required skilled artisans, which leads one to examine how fitz Osbern built Chepstow castle. Even from the beginning the undertaking of the project must have been prodigious and on a scale comparable to the building of, say, Dover castle, Windsor or the White Tower in London. Apart from the building material itself, the task would have called for the expert services of carpenters, stone masons and engineers. There would have also been a not inconsiderable force of labourers carrying the stone work, cutting the timber and mixing the mortar for the walls and digging the foundations. It was quite an accomplishment and a task which could have only been undertaken by an extremely wealthy man and one who was favoured by the king.

When William I died in 1087, it was to prove to be a significant year for both the Welsh and their would-be Norman masters. On the death of King William he was replaced by his son William Rufus, who would rule as William II. The Normans under their new king were not slow to capitalise on the continued tribal feuding between the various Welsh princes and used it to their advantage to spread dissent across the country and create disunity. They also realised how marriage between members of two important ruling families could benefit them as they sought to bring Wales under their control. One such political union came after 1087, when Bernard de Neufmarche (sometimes written as Newmarch), married one of the daughters of Gruffydd ap Llywelyn, the king of Gwynedd, in a marriage of alliance. Bernard de Neufmarche slowly but eventually advanced through the territories of Wye. In 1090 he was accompanied by Philip de Braose and, together with other Norman knights, they captured Radnor. Bernard de Neufmarche went on to seize Brycheniog and raise a castle at Brecon. By 1093 he was in Aberhonddu and beginning to wear down opposition in a process that was as much attrition as a military action. Through various liaisons were the Normans able to strengthen their control in Wales. These were ruthless times and anyone who stood against these powerful knights in warfare were invariably defeated. Some Welsh nobles, such as Rhys ap Tewdwr, tried to fight back but against the battle-experienced Norman troops, equipped with better weapons, they found the task very difficult. Rhys ap Tewdwr was killed in battle at Aberhonddu near Brecon in 1093 as he attempted to halt the Normans' continued advancement ever deeper into Wales. The event was recorded in the Brut, which relates how with his death: 'The kingdom of Wales has been overthrown'.

Five years later in 1098, another Welsh leader, Gruffydd ap Cynan, in league with Cadwgan ap Belddyn ap Cynfyn of Powys, hired a mercenary Viking fleet to sail from Dublin with the intention of helping them push back Fat Hugh, the earl of Shrewsbury, who had invaded Gwynedd. The Normans learned of this and bribed the Vikings to withdraw their support. Hugh was later killed in a separate incident against Vikings in Anglesey Sound. The Normans made a defensive withdrawal and an uneasy peace settled over Wales. Powys became the centre for the country's politics and Gruffydd and Cadwgan showed signs of becoming peaceable in their ways. Gruffydd especially became quiet, but he was biding his time and consolidating his position in Gwynedd.

William II was a petulant ruler given to making promises and then breaking them, making it hard to trust him. This trait led to him later losing any popularity he may have enjoyed when he first acceded to the throne. He argued with his barons and the Church, leading to a chronicler recording that William Rufus, so-called because of his red hair, was: 'A wicked, avaricious, evil-living man'. Another chronicler concluded that William was indeed: 'Wanton, lascivious and corrupt'. With the death of his father, he was not honour bound by any treaty made with the Welsh lords, but he did need the support of those Norman lords on the Welsh border. He was in awe of his father and tried on several occasions to emulate him. Yet, for all his faults, William was not a stupid man. He mounted two campaigns into Wales, the first being in 1095 and the second was conducted in 1097. Both were pursued with the intention of finally putting an end to the resistance in north Wales, but in the end they were unsuccessful and passed off without producing any results. The reason for this was simply because the Welsh refused to give battle to the Normans. Gerald of Wales in his work *The Description of Wales* remarks on this tactic which caused great irritation to the Normans:

> Although beaten today and shamefully put to flight, tomorrow they march out again, no whit dejected by their defeat or losses. They may not shine in open combat and in fixed formation, but they harass the enemy by their ambushes and night attacks. In a simple battle they are easily beaten, but they are difficult to conquer in a long war.

He was to be proven correct in this assessment and the Welsh would continue to be a problem for many kings. On both occasions when William II campaigned in Wales the local warriors, according to the Brut, 'sought a defence in their woods and their wildernesses'. With no riches or plunder to be gained in order to sustain his campaign, William was obliged to withdraw and his army 'returned home empty handed and having gained nought'.

The eleventh century closed with the death of King William II during a hunting party in the New Forest in the south of England. On the morning of 2 August 1100, the king was out hunting with a trusted friend, Walter Tirel, a soldier of fortune. Using crossbows to hunt their prey the two men separated to pursue different game. The king was mortally struck in the chest by an arrow shot from Tirel's crossbow. He did not remain at the scene of the accident and fled to France. This has led to accusations being levelled at William's brother Henry, who may have orchestrated the assassination. The truth will never be known, but certainly within hours of hearing of his brother's death, Henry rushed to Winchester where he seized the treasury. With the death of the first two Norman kings, the first phase of the Normans incursion into Wales came to an end. In Wales, the Brut remarked on William II's life and death by recording: 'he used concubines and because of that died without heirs'. The closing years of the eleventh century in Wales were a turbulent period, with Anglesey being granted to monks from Chester and castles being raised at Bangor and Caernarfon. Domesday Book also records that much of Powys was controlled by the Normans. But even so it was only a shadow of what was yet to come as under the reign of Henry the Normans would establish new lordships such as Gower and Gydweli in the southeast of the country and the Welsh would come to gain the much-needed experience in warfare and acquire the expertise and equipment required to successfully attack castles.

2

THE TWELFTH CENTURY

HENRY I: 1100–1135

In the closing years of the eleventh century, the Normans had made major moves into Wales, but the rebellion of 1094 made them realise that their new lands were far from being secure and the local populace were not subordinate to their will. The Welsh had managed to recover great swathes of lands in Dyfed, Ceredigion and Ystrad Tywi. Into this uncertain situation came the newly crowned King Henry I, about whom the Welsh knew little. New Norman lordships were created at Gower and Kidwelly (sometimes written as Gydweli) where a castle was also established by the king's ambitious minister Roger, bishop of Salisbury in 1106.

According to some historians, Henry I was a brusque and plain-speaking man *(12)*. This is a polite way of saying he was rude and coarse. If his brother William II had been promiscuous, Henry was to prove to be even more licentious in his ways, fathering two children in marriage and at least a further twenty illegitimate offspring. Despite his libidinous lifestyle Henry was to prove a strong and formidable king. He was to reign until 1135, but this Norman king was not without his own fair share of troubles within his court, in the form of his elder brother Robert, who was ruling territories in France as the duke of Normandy. Concerning the perennial question of Wales Henry decided he would try to control the country through the willing support of Welsh nobles, such as Hywel ap Gronw, acting as his allies. This created its fair share of anger and deepened resentment between the opposing sides, and many feuds were rekindled. For example one cannot help but think that Roger, bishop of Salisbury, was somehow involved in the murder of Hywel ap Gronw. It was by more than just coincidence that the lands of the king's murdered Welsh ally should be added to those already held by Roger. This was not an isolated incident and for the most part Welsh leaders had ulterior

12 King Henry I (1100–1135) was plain-speaking and had a brusque manner. He left his mark on Wales

motives in mind when they sided with the king and were acting purely out of self-interest.

Under King Henry I, castle building in England and Wales continued. One of the first to be built in Wales in the first year of his reign was at Oystermouth, between Swansea and Mumbles, in 1100. The castle would survive until 1215 when it was attacked and destroyed. This was followed in quick succession by a series of other castles such as Usk built by the powerful de Clare family in 1100 and Ogmore built around 1106 probably by Gwilim O'Lundein *(13 & 14)*. This century would also see the first influences of new castle designs being brought back to Britain by knights returning from the Crusades in the Middle East. One these new ideas was a feature called either hoarding (sometimes written as hourding) or bratticing, which is recorded as first being used in England *c.*1187, thereafter being used on some of the larger castles in Wales. Hoarding was a wooden construction which was fitted to the walls of castles as a type of scaffolding, thus allowing the defenders to rain missiles down on the attackers at the base of the walls. The method had long been in use in the Middle East and when applied to castles in Western Europe it would later develop into an integral stone structure called machicolations and become part of the castle walls. The early wooden keeps were being replaced by stone structures and termed 'shell keeps' and the wooden palisade walls of motte-and-bailey castles were replaced by stone constructions and termed 'curtain walls'. Cardiff castle, started in 1091, would develop along these lines to strengthen its

13 Ogmore castle built around 1106. It evolved from a motte-and-bailey style into a 'shell keep' with earthworks

14 The remains of the gatehouse at Ogmore castle, from a later period

defences. Castles were now taking on a formidable appearance as if to proclaim to the Welsh that the Normans were growing ever stronger. For example, in 1138 Gilbert de Clare, who as the first earl of Pembroke had ordered the building of a castle at Haverfordwest eighteen years earlier, also ordered the strengthening of the castle at Pembroke by building a keep some 75ft high with walls 19ft thick at the base. Not only was the architecture of the Norman castles taking on a very different appearance, the methods governing the way in which they were attacked was also changing. Special engines, referred to as artillery, were developed in order to hurl large stone projectiles and large, heavy-tipped arrows at the castle walls during siege operations. These would evolve into a range of devices known as ballista and perrier, with variations in size to permit a defending garrison to use such weapons from the walls of a castle. Tunnelling or mining was also developed whereby the attackers would seek to dig under the walls of a castle and special devices to hack away at the base of walls were being introduced. These were known as rams and their size would vary in accordance to the siege at which they were being used. The tried and proven methods of starving out the garrison and the use of fire still remained two of the most preferred ways of inducing a castle to surrender.

Henry I was a powerful and wise man and dealt with the Welsh in a sound manner. The Brut records him as being 'the man against whom none can contend save God himself'. This became evident in 1102 when Henry was moved to break the power of Robert of Beleme, who had lands stretching from mid-Wales to Maine in France. Robert of Beleme had enlisted the support of Cadwgan ap Blyddyn, the king of Powys, in an attempt to rebel against Henry. Becoming aware of this the king attacked and defeated the forces of Robert, who was exiled along with his brother Arnulf. To take his place in Dyfed Henry elected Gerald of Windsor, who had conducted the defence of Pembroke castle in 1094 and probably prevented the Normans from being evicted from Wales. Gerald would go on to build other castles in Wales, such as Cilgerran around 1110, which would later be developed into a formidable castle, withstanding two sieges *(15)*.

The authority which Cadwgan had once held over his vassals was undermined and in the face of internal strife his leadership became supplanted. In 1109 his son Owain abducted a lady by the name of Nest, who was the wife of Gerald of Windsor and the daughter of Rhys ap Tewdwr. For this act Cadwgan and Owain were both exiled. The marriage of Nest to Gerald had been arranged by Henry in a political move to unite the two societies, and her kidnapping by the Welsh could have led to an outright military campaign. By 1111 Cadwgan was once more in favour to the point where he planned the construction of one of the first castles to be built by a Welsh leader. The site was to be at Welshpool, but he was killed by his own nephew, Madog ap Rhirid, who had also killed Cadwgan's brother, Iorwerth, earlier in the same year. Internal fighting erupted between the two Welsh sides and lasted until

15 Cilgerran castle built around 1110 was besieged on at least two separate occasions

1115, when Cadwgan's son, Owain, finally defeated the last of his opponents to become established as the ruler of Powys. The first true castle to be built by the Welsh was eventually raised at Cymer near Dolgellau in 1116. Other castles would be built by the Welsh, initially built along the early design of the motte-and-bailey style. Eventually these would be replaced in the latter half of the twelfth century by more substantial castle designs such as Dolwyddelan, built at the head of the Conwy valley, near Betwys Y Coed, which would later become used as a royal seat.

Henry I was shrewd enough to realise the difficulties which lay ahead of him, especially those involved in attempting to conquer Wales where internal feuding threatened to unbalance the status quo. He resolved the problem by calling on the services of trusted Welshmen to govern parts of the country in his name. In effect, Henry was ruling Wales through figures known to the local populace and as such it would seem they were autonomous. In reality, Henry controlled these allies and could remove or place them in power with ease. During this period control of Deheubart passed into the hands of the princely house of Powys, while the Normans made cautious advances into the country. One of Henry's loyal subjects was Owain ap Cadwgan, whose earlier kidnapping of Nest was conveniently overlooked. In fact Owain was forgiven to the point where he is known to have travelled to Normandy with King Henry in

16 Carew castle, established by Gerald of Windsor to control the Teifi valley

1115 where he was knighted for his services. This was the first time any Welshman had had this honour bestowed on him. In 1116, in such a high position Owain, along with several other Welsh rulers, on behalf of Henry undertook to campaign against his fellow countryman, Gruffydd ap Rhys, the son of Rhys ap Tewdwr, who had been fighting against the Norman occupation for several years.

In 1109 the first royal castle was being raised at Carmarthen and it looked as though Henry was going to succeed in Wales where his father and brother had both failed. The year before, a number of Flemish immigrants had left Europe following a series of natural disasters and Henry was magnanimous enough to grant them permission to settle in south Dyfed. These were not considered military invaders but settlers and colonists and were referred to as the '*Landsker*'. Despite this claim, they proved to be 'at once industrious and warlike' and in order to protect themselves from attacks by the Welsh in this 'Little England beyond Wales' they erected a series of castles running from Narberth in the east to Roch in the west. One of these was Letterston, a motte-and-bailey design, built in the area of Pembroke. It was named after its Flemish builder, Letard Littleking, who would later be killed during fighting in 1137. Joining this influx came Robert fitz Martin from the West Country to establish the lordship of Cemais with a castle at Nevern. Gerald of Windsor by 1106 had established a castle at Carew with further outposts at Cenarth Bychan in the Teifi valley *(16)*. The Normans raised new castles at sites such as Llandovery and Kidwelly, both of which had at one time been motte-and-bailey defences.

The Welsh reaction to this level of activity was to take up arms against the Normans and in particular the *Landsker*. The main protagonist was Gruffydd ap Rhys, of Deheubarth, *c.*1100–1137, who viewed these incomers as yet more invaders of his country and began a campaign against them in 1116. He attacked and burned a number of sites including Narberth, Swansea and Llandovery, but he lacked the ability to undertake prolonged siege warfare and capture castles for his own use. Gruffydd was content to attack castles and destroy them, thereby denying them to the Normans. He used the most effective method available to him – burning the wooden structure of the castles, as many castles during this period were still undergoing a transitional stage from wood to stone buildings. The castle at Llandovery had only been established by Richard fitz Pons in 1116 when it was attacked by Gruffydd ap Rhys. His forces failed to enter the defences and only managed to burn the outer or bailey structure of the castle. When he attacked the castle at Narberth he had better luck and actually destroyed the site. It was not rebuilt until around 1215.

At the small site in Ystrad Peithyll, Gruffydd attacked using a combination of the two tactics at which the Welsh excelled. He attacked at night, something which was not normal in the conduct of war at that time, and using fire to set the buildings ablaze, Gruffydd's forces killed the garrison. The following day he moved on to attack and burn the castle at Aberystwyth, but Gruffydd was forced to withdraw when a large Norman force, led by Earl Gilbert fitz Richard, mounted a successful counter-attack. Gruffydd repeated his combination of fire and night attack at Carmarthen, where during the course of the fighting the constable of the castle, Owain ap Caradog, who had been loyal to Henry I, was killed. The castle held firm with only the outer castle or bailey being damaged by fire. At Blaenporth the castle, which had been built by Gilbert fitz Richard in 1110 and garrisoned by the Flemish settlers of the *Landsker*, was also burnt by Gruffydd's forces. The Brut chronicles the attack and records how he 'besieged the tower throughout the day, and many from the tower were slain'. Henry should have been worried by the largely successful actions of Gruffydd's forces, but he knew he could rely on his Welsh allies in the region, such as Owain ap Cadwgan, to attack on his behalf. Faced with an enemy force growing increasingly stronger, Gruffydd ap Rhys realised he had probably reached his limits and decided to withdraw into his ancestral lands where he lived out his days until his death in 1137. His short but bloody rebellion had little if any lasting impact on Henry's opinion of the way in which he should view or treat Wales.

Although Henry had been satisfied to use local Welsh rulers to do his bidding and maintain the peace, he was forced to mount two campaigns into Wales, the first being conducted in 1114 and the second completed in 1121. Neither were ever intended as true campaigns of conquest. Indeed, the first campaign was certainly intended to serve as a warning to Gruffydd ap Cynan, the lord of Gwynedd, that he should not overstep the mark of what convention allowed. It has long been claimed that the early campaigns mounted against the Welsh by the Norman kings did not have the objective of conquest in mind. It has been argued that such actions had a specific aim, which was to show the Welsh that the Normans were the power in the land. Certainly those conducted by William I and William II did not set out to conquer further territories in Wales, but instead to reaffirm the fact that the Normans could establish themselves wherever they chose.

When Henry personally led his campaign through Powys into the region of Gwynedd in 1114 it was in direct confrontation to Gruffydd ap Cynan, who had slowly but surely been consolidating a powerbase in such a manner as not to unduly alarm the king. However, Henry's loyal followers in Wales reported back to him and the decision was taken to mount an offensive in 1114. Gruffydd ap Cynan had taken up arms against the Normans in 1094 and had been imprisoned for his actions. For most Welsh lords, including Gruffydd who no doubt wished to avoid the full wrath of the king's retribution, this show of royal strength and determination was sufficient to make them realise that they had overreached their accepted position. Gruffydd ap Cynan paid a large sum of money to Henry, who accepted his submission and those of other Welsh rulers, including Owain ap Cadwgan and Maredudd ap Blydden. This once more brought stability, if for but a short period, to both north and south Wales. The campaign of 1121 conducted against Maredudd ap Bleddyn of Powys was aimed at curtailing his ambitions of expanding his power in the region. Henry's actions were entirely successful and Maredudd was once more forced to submit to the king.

For the greater part of his reign Henry's rule in Wales was never challenged seriously and he had control over the local populace and the Flemish *Landsker*. By 1135 he was sixty-seven years old, and he was showing no signs of weakness in his methods of ruling the country. In late November that year Henry was absent in France when word reached him that the Welsh were attacking the border regions into England and they had made many territorial gains. During the course of preparations for his return, the king was struck by a sudden and mysterious illness. He nevertheless went hunting sometime around 28 November and dined on a meal of lampreys, a dish of which he was particularly fond. His illness turned to fever and on 1 December 1135 Henry died. His legitimate children had pre-deceased him and the throne of England passed over to his nephew Stephen of Blois in 1135. Henry had been a strong king and his personality had kept order among the Normans and native Welsh

17 King Stephen wasted no time in claiming the throne, but he was a weak monarch and the Welsh used this fault against him

leaders. However, when he died violence erupted across Wales and there was much localised fighting between local rulers and attacks were made on Norman lords.

THE REIGN OF KING STEPHEN: 1135–1154

Stephen was crowned on 22 December 1135, three weeks after his uncle had died *(17)*. He was to prove a weak king and the Welsh soon discovered they could manipulate him. Indeed, Stephen's problems with Wales began only months into his reign. It was not only the Welsh who recognised Stephen's failings as king; even in England he was recognised as being a weak monarch and the Peterborough Chronicle recorded that when he acceded to the English throne: 'treason was soon in the land, for every man that could forthwith robbed another'. By 1136 matters really came to a head when Richard fitz Gilbert de Clare was murdered in April and Norman troops were defeated by a Welsh force led by Hywel ap Marredudd near Swansea. This was followed by an uprising of the Welsh led by Owain and Cadwaladr of Gwynedd, who invaded Ceredigion and forced the Normans to evacuate the region except for the garrison at Cardigan castle. A relief force dispatched by the Normans in October was attacked and defeated in battle at Crug Mawr. The Brut records

18   A scene from the siege of Carmarthen in 1145 when Gilbert fitz Gilbert de Clare captured the town

that the Welsh army included 'two thousand mailed horsemen ready for battle'. The Welsh were gaining experience and learning the new ways of fighting. In fact throughout Stephen's reign the Welsh were to remain a problem which could neither be ignored or resolved by military campaign.

When barely two years into his reign and Stephen found himself confronted by a civil war instigated by his cousin, Mathilda, the daughter of Henry I, which diverted his attention and forces, thus he could not afford to send as many troops as he may have liked in order to confront the uprisings in Wales. In fact, so severe was this uprising that it would not be until 1144 that Hugh Mortimer would succeed in regaining the area of Maelienydd and Gilbert fitz Gilbert de Clare taking Carmarthen in 1145 *(18)*.

In 1136 the Welsh began their attacks against castles, which were, after all, symbols of Norman domination. Castell Gwallter, a motte-and-bailey castle built by Walter de Bec in 1110 above the Leri valley, was attacked and captured by Cadwaladr and Owain of Gwynedd in 1136. They repaired the site, which would be held by their forces until sometime during 1154. Another motte-and-bailey castle to be attacked was Dinerth, built in 1110 by Gilbert fitz Richard to control the commote of Anhuniog. The Welsh employed their tried and proven tactic of setting fire to the wooden defences of the castle. The castle would change hands several times during the rest of the twelfth century, before finally being destroyed in 1208 by Maelgwn to prevent its use by his enemy Llywelyn Fawr. It never again enters Welsh Chronicles. In their attack on Cardigan castle in 1136 the forces of Cadwaladr and Owain failed to capture the site. Two years later they made another attempt, which also failed.

Another failure to capture a castle in the opening moves of the war against Stephen and his Normans came at Kidwelly, which was being held by the constable of the castle, Maurice de Londres *(20)*. It was an unusual attack in that it was led by Gwenllian, the wife of Gruffydd ap Rhys the lord of Deheubarth. She was the daughter of Gruffydd ap Cynan, the king of Gwynedd, and as such was no stranger to military actions. With her husband Gruffydd absent on a mission to seek reinforcements from his father-in-law, Gwenllian took it upon herself to attack Kidwelly castle with a force raised locally and including two of her sons, Morgan and Maelgwm *(19)*. The battle was fierce and the Norman defenders maintained control of the fight, during the course of which Morgan was killed. Gwenllian and her surviving son Maelgwn were captured along with a number of her followers. The Normans were particularly ruthless on this occasion and the prisoners were taken to a nearby field where they were all put to the sword. It was an act of terror intended to subdue the local populace through fear.

The Welsh maintained their pressure on the Normans and attacked a series of castles during 1137. The year also saw the death of Gruffydd ap Rhys, the husband of the recently killed Gwenllian, but their infant son, also called Rhys,

19 Above The stout walls of Kidwelly castle, which evolved into a design known as 'walls within walls' and proved enduringly strong

20 Left The gatehouse of Kidwelly castle, which was a formidable structure overlooking the estuary of the Tywi river

would grow up to become the ruler of Deheubarth and be called Yr Arglwydd Rhys, the Lord Rhys. Kidwelly castle would continue to feature prominently in the family history. Among those castles to be attacked in 1137 was Castell Humfrey, built in 1110 when Earl Gilbert invaded Ceredigion and Humfrey had seized the commote of Gwynionydd and built the castle above the Clettwr valley. The joint forces of Cadwaladr and Owain of Gwynedd successfully attacked and destroyed the defences, which were then abandoned. Some fourteen years later, Owain's son Hywel rebuilt the castle for his own use. In 1158 Castell Humfrey was attacked and captured by Roger de Clare. A Welsh force counter-attacked and according to chronicles 'slew the knights and other keepers who were there and won huge spoils and steeds and armour'. When the forces of Cadwaladr and Owain Gwynedd attacked the castle at Carmarthen, they burnt the defences, which would not be rebuilt until 1145 by Gilbert de Clare. It was then attacked by a Welsh force led by Cadell ap Gruffydd in 1146 who took up residency and rebuilt the defences for 'the strength and splendour of his kingdom'. It was to be short lived and Carmarthen was soon recovered by the Normans, who strengthened the castle to such an extent that it withstood at least two sieges conducted by Lord Rhys around 1159.

One of the most prominent Norman figures at this time was Gilbert fitz Gilbert de Clare, who had rebuilt Carmarthen and other defences. But with matters still far from settled in England Stephen was a troubled monarch. To add to his worries the Welsh still refused to be subdued easily. With leaders such as Owain and Cadwaladr Gwynedd, along with Madog ap Maredudd in Powys, showing they were capable of fighting back and were far from defeated by their military actions conducted against the Normans.

The fighting continued into the closing years of the 1140s, and the Normans built Ewloe castle near Hawarden in 1146. In the same year Owain Gwynedd, operating without his brother Cadwaladr, captured Mold castle. The castle at Llansteffan was attacked and taken by the combined forces of Cadell, Maredudd and Rhys ap Gruffydd, to show that the Welsh could co-operate in joint operations against the common enemy, which the Normans were, after all, to every Welshman. Maredudd then garrisoned the castle and held it against a Norman attack, which the Brut records:

> for a boy though he was in age, he showed none the less the action of a man...
> when the enemy saw how few were the defenders, they raised ladders against
> the walls, and he bore with his enemies until they were on the ladders, and then
> he came with his men and overturned the ladders, so that his enemies were in
> the ditch, many of them being slain and others put to flight.

Llansteffan castle would change hands a number of times during the rest of the twelfth century. This tripartite force maintained their pressure on the Normans and in 1147 they attacked the castle of Wiston, which had been founded by the Flemish *Landsker* during the reign of Henry I. It was a stoutly built defensible stone site and the garrison resisted the attackers. The attacking forces were 'too weak to master it', and the three men decided to turn to Hywel ap Owain, who was not viewed as a natural ally to their cause. Putting aside their differences Hywel aided the taking of Wiston by building 'certain battering engines'. Thus equipped, the combined force attacked the castle, which was seized with 'great toil and conflict'. This is an interesting development because this is among the earliest evidence that the Welsh had acquired the knowledge to build siege equipment, such as catapults and battering rams.

By 1150 Owain Gwynedd had defeated all opposition in Powys, including Welsh Normans, and he had reached the Cheshire borders. The Welsh also returned to localised feudal battles and in the three years between 1150 and 1153, Maredudd and Rhys ap Guffydd of Deheubarth had seized Ceredigion from the warriors of Gwynedd. With the Welsh fighting among themselves, the Normans had some respite from the wearisome battles with these unconventional people. One cannot help but think what would have happened had the Welsh resolved their differences and united to turn against the Normans. Had they called a truce among themselves there is every possibility they could have forced the Normans back, even if only for a short period, whilst they consolidated their forces and built up their strength. With his country ripped apart by civil war Stephen could not ignore the situation in England at that time. The Welsh had regained Gwynedd, Powys and Deheubarth and in 1151, three years before the death of Stephen, they had taken Tenby. This was in retribution against troops from Tenby who had made a personal attack on Cadell ap Gruffydd that left him crippled. The town was attacked at night and the garrison was put to the sword. Tenby would later be visited by Maelgwn ap Rhys, who burnt the town. In the same year the forces of Rhys ap Gruffydd moved to destroy the castle at Loughor which commanded the route between Swansea and Llanelli. Later, in 1260, Llywelyn ap Gruffydd added to the misery of Tenby when he attacked the town and set fire to buildings.

Throughout his reign Stephen's attention had been diverted, and this has led to him being called a weak king. Admittedly, on the face of the evidence available, he does not seem to have been able to concentrate on more than one problem at a time, which left him vulnerable to attack from both without and within his kingdom. During his reign it was written that for 'nineteen long winters ... God and his saints slept'. When he died in 1154 all the good achieved during the reign of his uncle, Henry I, had been undone, especially in Wales. Stephen died without a direct heir and the crown passed to Henry's grandson, who was also called Henry. An added irony was the fact that the boy had been born to Matilda, the daughter of Henry I, who had been the cause of so many problems in the early part of Stephen's reign.

21 King Henry II, a brave monarch for whom the Welsh had a sense of respect

THE REIGN OF HENRY II: 1154–1189

Although he was proclaimed to rule as Henry II in 1154, the new king postponed his ascension to the throne *(21)*. There were a number of reasons for this, including the fact that he sought to remedy the mistakes of Stephen. He also set out to regain his grandfather's authority in Wales, but in Owain of Gwynedd and Rhys of Deheubarth he found a pair of formidable enemies whom he was unable to wear down either through talks or action. Henry did achieve some early success in Wales and by 1155 he had Deheubarth under his control. In 1157 he set out from Chester to conduct a campaign against Owain ap Gwynedd, which was designed to force him away from the Chester border where he threatened English territory. The Welsh force was stronger than Henry's army and they sprang a traditional ambush and it seemed they would actually defeat the king. However, Henry personally led a force, which managed to turn the flank of the Welsh forces and Owain retired in good order. The two sides negotiated and Owain agreed to terms which saw him paying homage to Henry, who allowed him to march back to positions west of the Clwyd. But that was far from being the end of Rhys's resistance to Norman rule.

Henry II, as other Norman kings before him, had control of the seas. At the time of the land battle, a royal fleet sailed against Anglesey and attacked.

22 Drysllwyn castle, built on a hill with a commanding view overlooking the river Towy and surrounding area

The force was defeated when a landing was effected against the specific orders of the king. By this juncture Henry and Rhys had reached terms and were negotiating peace. By 1158 Henry had gained the submission of several Welsh princes, but Rhys of Deheubarth continued to fight back and even made significant gains. An attack against Cardigan castle in that same year showed the Normans that the Welsh were far from being a spent force. Another attack directed against Cardiff castle, led by Ivor Bach, resulted in its capture. These successes were re-emphasised when Walter Clifford, holding Llandovery castle, invaded Rhys's territory and prompted a retaliatory attack. Rhys seized the castle and held it. The castle was later retaken by the Normans and Henry spent a large sum of money on repairs and additions to its defences. Even so, that did not prevent its recapture by the Welsh, who managed to hold onto it until 1276. Indeed, the castle at Llandovery was to be fought over and held by each side a number of times during the thirteenth century before finally being used as a base of operations by Owain Glyn Dwr in the 1400s. At a number of castle sites water obstacles were beginning to feature quite prominently as defences. Being a natural feature it was relatively easy to incorporate a river into a castle's defences and many were sited to take advantage of this. For example, Pembroke castle had tidal access through the River Taf, which formed three sides of its defences. At Kidwelly and Laugharne the situation was similar, with tidal rivers affording both defence and a means of allowing resupply by ship. Even those castles at Cardigan and Carmarthen could be supplied by ships navigating the Rivers Teifi and Towy respectively. The castles at Drysllwyn and Newcastle Emlyn were built on hills overlooking the Rivers Towy and Teifi respectively *(22 & 23)*. Whilst their elevated positions prevented water being incorporated directly into their defences the close proximity of this obstacle did afford a degree of safety from attack in the area through which the rivers flowed.

In 1163 Henry II was forced to campaign in Wales again, his fourth such operation since 1158. This action had been prompted by Rhys's forces, who had captured Llandovery in 1162. The campaign was a short one and Rhys was captured at Pencader and taken to England. Along with Owain Gwynedd he paid homage to Henry II at the town of Woodstock, for which act the king restored Rhys's lands to him. However, it was a short-lived peace because the fighting started again in 1164 when Rhys attacked Ceredigion and joined forces with Owain Gwynedd. Henry faced total insurrection throughout Wales as other Welsh leaders joined together against him. These included Owain Cyfeiliog and Iowerth Goch of Powys, and Cadwallon ap Madog and Einion Clud from south Wales.

23 Newcastle Emlyn, built to command the river Teifi. It would evolve into a formidable site with earthworks and stout gatehouse

Henry's earlier campaign had been well planned, but in 1165 he was to find himself faced with great adversity and determination from the Welsh, as well as inclement and unseasonal weather conditions. Henry started his campaign from Oswestry and moved into Powys with the plan of crossing the Berwyn mountains. Halfway across this featureless plateau, which rises to more than 800m in places, his army was engulfed by torrential rains and driving winds. These were the terrain and weather conditions in which the Welsh excelled in fighting. In a mountainous pass at Corwen they surrounded his encampment and from the heights attacked him with great ferocity. Henry's army fell into disarray and fled with great losses. With his advance hampered by the weather and the unconventional methods of Welsh attacks, he realised he could make no headway into Wales and was forced to withdraw. Had Henry continued there is evidence to show that Owain Gwynedd had deployed his forces at Hawarden in preparation to meet the king in open battle again as he had in 1157. In the event the two sides never met and given the Welsh ability to learn through their actions, there is every possibility that Owain's forces might have triumphed. Certainly, had Henry continued through the severe storms his men would have been in no fit condition to fight a battle, especially after being routed at Corwen. In the meantime Rhys ap Gruffydd had not been idle and his forces captured Cardigan castle and Cilgerran castle, which were to remain under Welsh control until 1204.

Owain Gwynedd was the natural leader of this uprising and with the close support of Rhys they maintained the pressure against Norman rule in Wales. Rhys was a tactician of the old ways, believing in guerrilla warfare methods and quick victories. However, he had learned ways of dealing with Norman cavalry on the battlefield and also how to attack, capture and hold castles. He was quick to take advantage of this and even improve the defences of those he captured, to the point where they were held for many years by the Welsh. Together Rhys and Owain had instigated Henry's campaigns, and were very obviously the bane of his life. The two Welsh leaders remained closely allied and in 1167 they attacked and captured Rhuddlan after a siege lasting three months. Owain attacked and destroyed Basingwerk castle and extended his control into the area of the Dee. When he died in 1170, Henry's problems with the Welsh were immediately halved.

Henry II in the meantime had come to realise that with the failure of his campaign in 1164–1165 his attitude towards the Welsh had to be more accommodating. He therefore decided on compromise with Rhys and accepted his position and power. For the remainder of Henry's reign Rhys would continue to be a powerful Welsh leader and build his own castles. One of these was Cardigan castle, which was rebuilt 'in stone and mortar' in 1171. Henry's popularity in England was extremely low and he became isolated after he was implicated in ordering the murder of Thomas Becket in 1170. His decision to invade Ireland in 1171 left him with fewer supporters. Seeking to gain favour, Henry met with Rhys at Laugharne castle where he created him the king's justiciar (chief political and judicial officer) in south Wales. He was now Lord Rhys of Deheubarth and the lesser rulers in south Wales and northern Glamorgan were under his protection. He held court at Cardigan and Dinefwr in the Tywi valley and through him Henry was ruling Wales in a manner akin to his grandfather, Henry I. However, it was too little too late. When the king's sons turned on their father between 1173 and 1175, Rhys became personally involved when he sent one of his sons and Welsh rulers from the south to support Henry. The damage to Henry's reputation was done and resentment of the Normans was never going to abate.

In fact an example of just how cruel and treacherous the Normans could be was shown in 1175 when the king's vassal, William de Braose, succeeded to the lordship of Abergavenny castle which had been built between 1087 and 1100. Such was the notoriety of this infamous knight, who 'relished in wickedness', that he was known across Wales. Even during the turbulent power struggle which raged between the Normans and the native Welsh, the vile wickedness of de Braose stood out. In December 1175 de Braose perpetrated one of his most heinous crimes. He invited the influential Welsh leader, Seisyll ap Dyfnwal, (sometimes written as Sitsyllt ap Dyfnwal) along with his son Geoffrey and a number of their Welsh warriors, to a great feast at Abergavenny castle. During the meal the Welsh were murdered and de Braose moved on to the nearby Arnold castle (sometimes written as Castell Arnallt), the family seat of Seisyll, and murdered his wife and the rest of his family, including his young son Cadwaladr. The action was in vengeance for the death of de Braose's uncle by a member of Seisyll's family. Several years later, Welsh forces attacked Abergavenny castle and stormed it using ladders to scale the walls. According to the historian Gerald of Wales, the Welsh 'burned the place down'. Following these events and others, a Chronicler of the Brut records how 'none of the Welsh dared place their trust in the French'. The fighting between the two cultures was far from being at an end.

Despite de Braose's murderous act and many others committed by the Normans, Rhys and Daffydd ab Owain Gwynedd travelled to Oxford in 1177 to pay homage to the king. The special relationship enjoyed between King Henry and Rhys was strained many times, such as when fighting broke out in Cardiff and Kenfig in 1185. These actions threatened the relationship, but their close ties held and apart from localised fighting there was no need for further large-scale actions into Wales. When Henry died in 1189, however, all that was to change.

Out of a reign lasting thirty-four years, Henry II had been absent from his kingdom for twenty-one years, preferring instead the social and cultural circles in Europe. He had tried to bring about a solution with Wales, but even in the year of his death the Welsh were still attacking and seizing Norman castles. Upon the death of the old king it was almost as if the special relationship between Henry and Rhys had never been and war broke out almost immediately. One of the first to take up arms was Rhys himself, who led several attacks on Norman strongholds. For example, at St Clears near to the Rivers Cynin and Taf, he mobilised his forces to capture the castle. It was later to be retaken by the Normans, but the forces of Llywelyn ap Iowerth were to capture it again in 1215.

THE REIGN OF RICHARD I: 1189–1199

Richard succeeded as king on the death of his father, Henry II *(24)*. He was destined to rule for ten years, but in all that time he spent only six months in England. For the remainder of his reign Richard served on campaign in the Crusades. In fact, it was whilst he was returning to England from a Crusade in 1292 that he was taken prisoner and held for ransom in Austria. For fourteen months, from December 1292 until February 1294, he was kept captive until two-thirds of a 150,000-mark ransom was paid. He was a strong and brave king; his courage was without question, which led to him being called 'Richard the Lionheart'. This courage also led to him being headstrong and impetuous, inclined to take more risks than necessary. In April 1199, Richard was engaged in besieging the castle of Chalus-Chabrol near Limoges, which was part of his campaign to suppress a revolt by French nobles, when he was struck by an arrow fired from a crossbow. The wound became infected and he died, leaving the crown of England to be passed to his foolish and often wicked brother John, who would rule from 1199 to 1216.

It was not long after the death of Henry II that war broke out in Wales, due in most part to the offhand manner in which Richard, as the new king, dealt with Rhys ap Gruffydd. Had he taken a different approach towards Rhys and renewed the relationship enjoyed between the Welsh leader and the late king, Richard may have maintained the peace, no matter how strained at times, and prevented much unrest between Wales and England. In the event, Rhys wasted no time and seized the opportunity to increase his power. In other parts of the country the Welsh did not hesitate and the lordships of Cemaes and Kidwelly were taken, and by 1194 Carmarthen itself was seized.

The reason for Richard being absent from his kingdom in England was the fact that he was more absorbed by events in his territories on the Continent, such as Aquitaine. He also embarked on Crusades, which meant his kingdom was left to be ruled in his absence by his brother, Prince John, and barons and earls, some of whom had principles of a rather questionable nature. However, for the main part the natural course of events continued to unfold as though he were present.

Castles were still being built, such as the one at Picton, erected in 1190 by William de Picton, a Norman knight, to the south-west of Haverfordwest.

24 King Richard I, a brave monarch but he only spent six months of his ten-year rule in England. He died in France after service in the Middle East on campaign during the Crusades.

Added to this were those built by the Welsh, such as Dinefwr and Rhayader, along with others *(25)*. The region of Gwynedd was at this time a part of Wales without Norman settlement and the most remote area away from the sphere of Norman influence. Therefore, the princes of Gwynedd were able to build stone castles at sites such as Dolwyddelan, Dolbarden and Criccieth, built by Llywelyn Fawr and Llwelyn ap Iowerth respectively *(26)*. These structures replaced earlier wooden-and-earth castles, like Daffydd ab Owain's castle at Rhuddlan. The new castles were designed to make Gwynedd a safer area through which to travel and in which to take up residency. They were simple but strong in design and had the desired result.

On 24 December 1193 the methods used by the Welsh to attack castles suddenly took on a new direction and became a strategic action. On that date it is recorded how 'the war band of Maelgwyn ap Rhys [the illegitimate son of Lord Rhys] manfully breached the castle of Ystrad Meurig with slings and catapults.' This is an interesting development in the history of Welsh castles at war because for the first time we learn that Welsh forces were beginning to equip themselves with the means to attack castle walls in the form of engines designed specifically for siege warfare. This period was also a time for family disputes to be settled along with many campaigns being conducted with small but effective armies. But not all fighting involved castles or used the massed and serried ranks of armies. Some actions stemmed from dissent among the

25   Dinefwr castle, built in the late twelfth century during a building programme of castles intended to bring about control over the Welsh

26   Criccieth castle, built by Llwelyn ap Iowerth and one of the first stone castles to be erected by a Welsh ruler

local populace, as at the battles of Porthaethwy and Coedanau in 1194. These were fought between Llywelyn ab Iowerth, born in 1173 and later to become better known as either Llywelyn Fawr or Llywelyn the Great, and his uncle, Daffydd ab Owain of eastern Gwynedd, whom he defeated. In 1195 the now-ageing Lord Rhys was challenged by his sons Rhys and Maredudd, but he still had sufficient power to have them imprisoned, rather ironically, in Ystrad Meurig castle. Later Maelgwyn would return to this site in 1208 and complete its destruction by burning it, to prevent its occupation by Llywelyn ab Iorwerth.

The closing years of the twelfth century were extremely turbulent in Wales and events were unfolding at a rapid pace. In spite of his advancing years Lord Rhys continued to attack a number of Norman lordships along the borders. In 1196 the Norman justiciar, Hubert Walter, laid siege to a castle in Welshpool in the Powys area which had been built by the local princes. In 1197 it was re-taken by Gwenwynwyn ab Owain, prince of southern Powys and Powys Wenwynwyn. The king, or rather those ruling in his absence, were beginning to adopt an aggressive policy towards Wales and the fear of alienation in their own lands created among the Welsh a spirit to fight on against imposed rule from a Norman king. An attack on Wiston castle was led by Hywel Sais who gained access to the castle 'by treachery' and Philip fitz William and his family were imprisoned. It seemed that the Welsh were still prepared to employ unscrupulous methods to seize castles, as well as siege engines. In 1197 Lord Rhys died and left behind a power vacuum which had to be filled. Whether his place would be taken by a Welsh ruler with Norman affiliations or a true patriotic Welshman remained to be seen. Certainly among his sons there was much arguing and Deheubarth remained splintered. After much wrangling Rhys's sons separated and went their own ways. Further disputes and infighting saw the country being divided, with the balance of power moving to the north. In this weakened state any form of resistance to the Normans was quickly and easily dealt with. For example, a Welsh army was destroyed at Painscastle by Geoffrey fitz Peter in 1198.

King John assumed the throne in 1199 and almost at once gave his support to Llywelyn ab Iorwerth, the grandson of Owain Gwynedd. Llywelyn had earlier fought his uncles to successfully claim his inheritance and now he was receiving royal favour from the king himself. However, as events would prove, John would have cause to regret his decision. This particular Llywelyn was a powerful figure and by 1200, most of the area of Gwynedd was under his control, which only added to his reputation. In 1204 he married King John's illegitimate daughter, Joan, in order to maintain his royal connections. But, that too would fall apart as events took a different course and John embarked on a series of campaigns against the Welsh.

27   Re-enactment of how an attack might have looked. This depicts an attack on a wooden stockade on a motte or hillock. There would have been much hand-to-hand fighting

BATTLE TACTICS OF THE WELSH

Attack on a Castle

Gerald of Wales recorded that the Welsh tactic of 'hit and run' was not conducted out of tactical brilliance but more to a lack of understanding the art of war and probably no more than simple cowardice. This is a rather unfair assessment because in their initial attack in battle the Welsh were a formidable force. But if they did not break the enemy with their first attack they had the tendency to disintegrate and their army lose its coherency. Further resistance to their force led to them withdraw and seek safety, consolidating for another action at some time in the future.

In the days before the advent of gunpowder the strength of any castle lay in its protective walls; providing these were stout enough and well maintained they could withstand most forms of attack and the garrison was fairly secure. At first the Welsh lacked the resources to directly assault those castles held by the English. However, through the experiences of Welshmen fighting in France and the Crusades they soon learned the new tactics and adopted the methods required to attack castles. The English had already had the technology required to lay siege to castles and they also had the manpower and finances to undertake such a strategy. Furthermore, the English soldiers had time because, unlike the local Welsh people, they did not have to tend livestock or crops to harvest. For the Welsh it would be a question of time and learning through hard lessons on the battlefield *(27)*.

The local armies raised in Wales during the eleventh century to oppose the Normans would have not been much different from those deployed by King Harold at the battle of Hastings in 1066. The armour, weapons and personal equipment would have been of a similar style; the only real difference would have lain in the size of the force and the tactics they employed. The Welsh displayed a preference for using unconventional tactics, of a style which today would be termed guerrilla warfare. But over 900 years ago such ambush and hit-and-run tactics were regarded as being unworthy of any opponent.

Firm evidence regarding battle plans used by the Welsh forces at this time is very scant, but from what does exist one can build up a fairly reliable picture. The size of an army could vary from a few hundred, which would comprise a raiding party, to probably never more than 3,000 men. Under the military laws as laid down by Hywel Dda, a tenth-century Welsh king, only freemen could actually take part in direct fighting. These laws stated that the ruler of a kingdom might raise taxes to support his army, which could include men as young as fourteen years old, providing they were freemen. They were to be supported in time of war by Bondsmen, who were precluded from fighting on account of their social status. Instead they served by carrying supplies of weapons, food and other support for the army.

It is more than likely that whilst freemen had a duty to serve in the army, they would have received little if anything in the way of formal military training. Most would probably gain their first experience of battle during their first engagement. Strange as it may seem, this policy was actually more widely practised than one would believe, being used in other European states of the time.

The freemen formed the central core of the fighting force, but in addition the leader would have his own personal bodyguard, called a *Teulu*, much the same as the Housecarls who had served Harold at the battle of Hastings. The members of this elite unit were completely loyal to their king and were close to him at all times. They served for six weeks out of every year, which, although it does not sound like a long period, was sufficient when conducting cross-border raids into neighbouring territories or into England. The Welsh also realised that by only allowing freemen to fight, their losses in battle would reduce this group within the structure of their society. To this end they bolstered their fighting forces by using the services of mercenaries. In fact, mercenaries feature in Welsh military history, usually Vikings from settlements in Ireland, before, during and after the Norman Conquest.

The tactics the Welsh troops employed in battle were not well co-ordinated and were more akin to headlong rushes directly at the enemy's positions. This

28 Re-enactor showing how a mounted Norman knight might have looked with mail armour

29 Re-enactor depicting a Norman foot soldier, armed with sword and 'kite-shaped' shield and wearing a conical helmet with nasal guard

was not in keeping with the more stringent, well-disciplined military regime of the Saxon or Norman armies, who would stand their ground and hold as a cohesive force. They realised the value of strength in numbers and supporting one another in battle. Against this the Welsh preferred a less subtle approach and were more fluid on the battlefield. It was not a question of not being able to stand and fight, they could certainly do that when the need arose, it was simply that short, but fierce blows against the enemy were the preferred Welsh style. This tactic could produce a quick, decisive victory, or if the enemy were too resolute, they could withdraw very fast. In short, these tactics were best suited to ambushing an enemy on the march, because the more heavily armoured Norman knights with their large 'kite-shaped' shields were imbued with the spirit of standing and fighting *(28)*. What is certain is that such ambush tactics worked and took a steady toll in lives.

Over the years this tactic of giving ground came to be the standard practice of the Welsh as they realised that they did not possess the wherewithal to

30 Re-enactor as a mounted Norman knight armed with lance and wearing mail armour and helmet. He would have been a formidable opponent in the open, but in the Welsh hills he lost the advantage

31 Re-enactor showing how a Saxon warrior would have looked. Welsh troops would have had a similar appearance with helmets being brought in from various centres of production

engage the Normans in their customary set-piece battles *(29)*. It is not surprising that this was the case, considering their isolation from the main influences of military thinking. However, discretion being the better part of valour, these bands of warriors may have preferred the adage of 'he who runs away lives to fight another day'. Certainly this was true when it came to their assessment by Gerald of Wales (also referred to as Geraldis Cambrensis, who was born at Manorbier castle in 1146). He was a great scholar and wrote many historical references to the Welsh and their attitude towards warfare.

Rather than being seen as a weakness, this refusal to give battle against a larger army with better equipment and training, and about whom the Welsh knew little, was actually part of the military doctrine of the great Chinese military thinker Sun Tzu, dating from the fifth century BC. In fact, it was this very refusal to give battle which made the Welsh so difficult to subdue.

Another tactic employed by the Welsh was to use the cover of night to launch surprise attacks. This again was unheard of in Saxon or Norman military society, who viewed the practice of attacking one's enemy in the darkness of night as being completely unchivalric. The Welsh, however, were opportunists and night attacks were, for them, just an extension of their guerrilla warfare tactics, which they employed to good effect to cover their movements. Even those who knew or were aware of such unconventional warfare, were often taken aback by the suddenness of night attacks.

Personal armour protection for the ordinary Welsh foot soldier, apart from probably a conical helmet and a round shield, was largely unused *(30)*. It was only later, when mail armour shirts were stripped from dead Norman troops that Welsh warriors were able to equip themselves with light armour and better weapons. Only the richest nobles would have had the means and resources to acquire the best in mail armour through trading centres such as Chester or Dublin. The shields used by the Welsh were of the round type with a raised central boss, and whilst practical they did not offer the same level of protection as the Norman 'kite' shields, which if formed into walls allowed them to shelter from the hails of arrows *(31)*. The round shield left parts of the body vulnerable, especially the legs, which were exposed to the cutting actions of swords.

The Welsh warriors used a variety of weapons ranging from swords and axes through to spears and bows. These would have come from many different sources, including being taken from the Norman dead. Weapons were also made locally at sites in Wales that were rich in the mineral deposits, such as iron and copper, required for their manufacture *(32)*. The longbow at this time was not of the style which would come to be used with such devastating effect during the Hundred Years War, but in the twelfth century it was the standard from which that would eventually evolve. The Welsh longbow differed from existing bows of a similar design by having a longer body. This allowed the archer to draw the bowstring back to his cheek, rather than just his chest. This method had a two-fold effect. Firstly, it allowed the archer to take better aim at his intended target. Secondly, it provided greater range and power, and the penetrative capabilities became legendary. To draw the bowstring of such a bow required a man to apply a pull of some 70lbs and much practice had to be put into gaining experience with such a weapon. The medieval historian, Gerald of Wales, tells how the men of Gwent used 'bows made of wild elm, unpolished, rude and uncouth, not only calculated to shoot an arrow to a great distance, but also to inflict very severe wounds in close fight.'

Stories were told how a Welsh archer could pierce 4 inches of oak with the arrow from his bow. Other tales abounded of how Norman knights were pinned to their saddles by Welsh archers, whose arrows had penetrated the mail armour. Whether legend or fact, the truth was that the Normans came to dread the Welsh archer.

Whilst men from the south favoured the bow, Gerald of Wales tells us how the Welsh warriors in the north around Snowdon and Merioneth preferred the

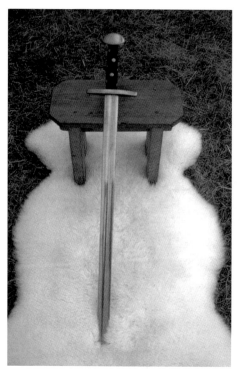

32 Above left Recreated sword of the period, showing the long straight blade. It was a simple yet effective design and could inflict heavy wounds in battle

33 Above right Recreated examples of maces, long and short handle styles, with a light axe. These were alternative weapons for foot soldiers or mounted troops. The long-handled mace was preferred by mounted troops for the extended reach

34 Right Heavier-style axe for use by foot soldiers against mounted troops. This is recreated but based on an authentic design of the period

35 Re-enactor showing the longbow being readied for use. He wears a helmet and padded jacket, as would have been the style

spear. This made them capable of acting as a cohesive unit capable of closing with the enemy for close-quarter fighting, rather than striking at a distance as with the archers. Swords and axes were also close-quarter weapons which could be used to inflict severe wounds, especially the axe which could crush bone *(33)*.

There would have been no finesse to fighting with swords, which would all have been of the long-bladed style with a cross-hand guard and stout handle ending in a pommel of varying style, but usually round in shape. The swords were of Viking influence with long, straight blades tapering to a point. These weighed around 4lbs or 5lbs and were well balanced. If a man had his sword arm broken by the blow from an opponent yielding such a weapon he was usually as good as dead, because he could no longer defend himself. Short-bladed knives and daggers were sometimes used, but generally speaking it was the larger, heavier weapons which were used in battle. The short-bladed weapon with a single edge carried by the Welsh was called a scramasax. It was worn on the belt and could be considered more of a tool than a true weapon of war *(34)*.

On their arrival in England in 1066, the Normans found the Saxon style of fighting on foot rather strange to comprehend, because they were largely a mounted force. They relied on horses for mobility and as a shock arm to attack and pursue enemy infantry units. The Welsh did have horses, but these were of the short-legged, stocky breed indigenous to the country. They could in no way be used as proper cavalry mounts in the same way as the Normans, who had bred horses selectively for this purpose. The local Welsh horses, therefore, were best used for moving riders with relative ease from one area to another and not for direct battle.

The Normans found out to their great cost how the difficult terrain of the country took a steady toll on the health and endurance of their horses. Cavalry charges, when they were made against Welsh foot soldiers, usually petered out as the locals retreated deep into the rugged hills. Again, Gerald of Wales writes how 'the Gallic style' of the armoured knight was too heavy for this new style of warfare and thus they could not follow the retreating force easily. This, then, rendered virtually useless the Norman's main shock tactic on the battlefield. Despite this, they were still on occasion able to utilise the mounted cavalry, but with limitations. Even the Norman foot soldiers were too heavily encumbered to follow the Welsh into the hills, despite the insistence of their commanders in the field.

From this outline assessment, the varying styles of warfare and difficulties experienced by both Welsh and Normans can be determined. It can also be ascertained that in the eleventh century the Welsh possessed limited means of attacking the early Norman castles, even though they were only of the motte-and-bailey style. It would not be until the latter half of the twelfth century that they would obtain the heavy equipment and sufficient experience to pose any kind of threat to a Norman castle and bring it under siege conditions. This would only come to them through their fellow countrymen who had fought in the European wars of the English kings. Their experiences would hone Welsh tactics for attacking castles and fighting an enemy in open warfare. The English for their part would continue to make use of Welshmen to provide archers equipped with the formidable longbow *(35)*. For example, at the battles of Crécy, Poitiers and Agincourt large numbers of Welshmen would be found among the archers who decimated the very elite of the French knights who fell under their hail of arrows.

3

THE THIRTEENTH CENTURY

KING JOHN AND LLYWELYN AP IORWERTH

The Welsh princes may well have argued among themselves but the unique form of diplomacy they developed would see them reaching an agreement between themselves when it suited them. They had also learned how to use any disunity among the English to their own advantage. They had used this during the reign of Stephen (1135–1154) and would use it again during the reign of Edward II (1307–1327). The Welsh princes and leaders would conspire with disloyal or disaffected barons in order to gain concessions, as happened during the reign of King John *(36)*. On the other hand, when a strong king ruled, such as Edward I (1272–1307) they would agree or submit to many or all entreaties made of them.

When King Richard died in 1199 he left no legitimate heirs to follow him as direct successor. In view of this, the crown passed to his brother John, who had taken it upon himself to rule England during Richard's absence when on Crusade. He was to prove an unpopular and weak king, often making wrong decisions. The Welsh were quick to realise this and use it against him in their continued resistance to the Anglo-Norman monarchy. On accession to throne he also inherited territories in France and for the first three years of his reign he spent most of his time in these possessions. Although he was personally in charge, events did not go the way the king would have liked. John made unwise military decisions and by 1203 he had lost all his lands in France. This led to him being called 'John Softsword', while before he had been known as 'John Lackland'. He returned to England, but his problems were compounded by the fact that he argued with the Church and his ministers. Indeed, John was deeply suspicious and trusted few in his court. He was still viewed as a Norman like other English kings before and as such was never popular, and the taxes he levied on the populace only served to widen this division.

36 King John: an unwise and suspicious
monarch, he tried to negotiate with the
Welsh, but when that failed he campaigned
into Wales, which was also a costly failure

At the same time as he was losing his territories in France, John was fortunate enough to have a time of relative stability in Wales. John probably understood the Welsh better than he has been given credit for, because he had at one time been lord of Glamorgan. Through this knowledge he was able to reverse the tables on the Welsh and, when necessary, set them against one another. In this he emulated Henry II and through offers of power and position he was able to secure support from many Welsh leaders, which he would use for his own end. With such serious actions taking place on the Continent, the king obviously wanted to keep some kind of order in Wales. To this end John entered into a formal written treaty with Llywelyn ap Iorwerth of Gwynedd, the first such between an Anglo-Norman king and a Welsh ruler, whereby along with a number of other native leaders they would swear fealty to the king. However, it was not the first time the two men had engaged in discussions. In 1200 Llywelyn had enjoyed the king's support, before having it taken away in a fickle moment. The following year the king had another change of mind and once more gave his support to Llywelyn. The bond between the two leaders was strengthened in 1204 when Llywelyn married John's illegitimate daughter Joan. The family unity was to last for several years until Llywelyn's dealings with the disgraced William de Braose angered John, who turned on his son-in-law. In 1211 the king would mount two campaigns into Wales with the intention of putting an end to Llywelyn's obviously growing power.

Llywelyn ap Iorwerth was born around 1173 and began his rise to prominence by defeating his uncles in battle between 1194 and 1202. By the time of his death in 1240 he would become known as Llywelyn Fawr, 'Llywelyn the Great' and have built a number of castles across the country. These included Ewloe, several miles from Hawarden, Criccieth and Dolbarden, all of which added to his power, along with Dolwyddelan, which guarded the route between the Vale of Conwy and Ardudw. Another castle he raised was Castell Y Bere, set in the Cadair Idris Range, built around 1220, four years after the death of King John. It would later play a significant part in the Welsh Rebellion of 1282–1283. In 1208 Llywelyn attacked and conquered Powys, seizing it from Gwenwynwyn, who was, in any case, not in favour with John. Llywelyn went on to take Cardigan, by which time his actions were beginning to alarm the king, who was concerned at his son-in-law's continued rise in power. Llywelyn's dealings with William de Braose were too much for the king and he was left with no other option than to take direct action.

Over the next eight years, until the time of John's death in 1216, the Welsh would attack many castles, including Kidwelly, which was destroyed in 1215, and Dinefwr. Many of the castles in Wales at this time were still undergoing a transitional phase from the original motte and bailey to a design incorporating stone walls and buildings. For example, Pembroke castle was still partially earthworks where stone defences had only begun to appear at the end of the thirteenth century. These included flanking towers to provide cover to vulnerable sections of the curtain walls. Such towers were at first square in design, but later they would develop into round towers because this design left fewer blind spots which could not be observed by sentries.

A show of strength was needed to remind Llywelyn that he was subject to the king's rule. In May 1211 John embarked on his first campaign, setting out from Chester. However, it was not properly organised and had to be withdrawn due to lack of supplies. By July, the king was ready for another campaign; this time he was better provisioned and with the support of many Welsh lords, who were equally alarmed at Llywelyn's growing power. The force marched from Oswestry to Bangor and were able to bring all that territory under their control. John also built castles during this period, including that at Aberystwyth, which would later be extended by Edward I. Greatly weakened by this assault, Llywelyn was forced back into Snowdonia and, left with no other choice, he sued for peace. The ruler of Gwynedd forfeited his lands between the Rivers Conwy and Dee, and he paid an enormous fine in horses and cattle. It was also agreed that should Llywelyn die with no heir to succeed him from his marriage to Joan, then his remaining lands would become property of the crown.

Counting on the continued support from loyal Welsh leaders, it was John's intention to capitalise on his success and he began to install officials into positions of office across Wales. This greatly annoyed his Welsh allies and had the effect of causing them to reverse their loyalties and seek to align themselves with Llywelyn of Gwynedd. In 1212 John intended to campaign across the whole of Wales and for this purpose he recruited troops from Scotland, Ireland and Flanders. It was a large army, including a force of some 8,000 engineers alone, whose job it would have been to tunnel under the walls of castles during siege operations. They would also be required to construct the powerful siege engines, such as the mangonel and Perrier to batter the walls with heavy stone projectiles *(37, 38 & 39)*.

With such a formidable force at his disposal, John looked set to achieve in Wales what other kings before him had failed. It would take time, but the campaign to begin the final conquest of Wales seemed to be on the point of being imminently launched. Faced with such a powerful army, Llywelyn entered into a treaty with Philip Augustus of France and signed an agreement guaranteeing mutual support in the event of an attack by the English king. At this stage of proceedings, the king's daughter Joan learned of a plot to kidnap her father by the Welsh or his own disloyal barons. On learning of this the king abandoned his campaign. Whether or not the information was true, the delay had bought the Welsh some time in which to prepare themselves. By 1213 fighting between the Welsh and Normans was growing in intensity, with both sides mounting attacks against castles. One of the first castles to be attacked was Dinefwr, which was being held for the Welsh by Rhys Grug, who was himself no stranger to siege warfare, having captured the castle at Llandovery in 1210. The attacking force was led by Rhys Ieuancy, ironically the nephew of Rhys Grug, who was loyal to King John and had a number of Norman troops under his command.

The action was fiercely fought and possession of the castle greatly contested. In the end, the attacking forces seized the castle, but it was at a great price in troops. According to one account:

> on the first assault the whole castle was taken, except for the tower. And in that all the garrison gathered together and they defended strongly with missiles and stones and other engines, and from without archers and cross-bow men were shooting missiles, and sappers digging, and armed knights making unbearable assaults, till they were forced before the afternoon to surrender the tower.

From this it will be seen that close-quarter action in confined spaces was now developing as a tactic for fighting. Engineers were tunnelling under the walls so as to cause them to collapse, thereby creating a breach in the walls through which the attackers could assault.

After 1216 Llywelyn would present Dinefwr castle to Rhys Grug, obviously as a reward for his support against King John's forces. By 1220, however, Rhys would dismantle the defences, apparently in order to prevent Llywelyn from using the castle for his own purposes. It would later be repaired and play a part

37 Above left   A recreated
Perrier siege engine of the
medieval period. It is seen here
being prepared for use

38 Above right   A recreated
Perrier, a catapult operated by
men hauling on ropes to supply
the momentum to hurl the
stone projectile, seen here
loaded with a stone projectile
and ready to launch

39 Left   A recreated Perrier
catapult at point of launching
its stone projectile. They were
simple yet effective in siege
operations

40 Llanstephan castle, attacked by Llwelyn ap Iowerth and captured, thereby proving that the Welsh could attack and hold a castle

in the wars of 1257 and continue in military service until the fourteenth century.

In 1214 King John suffered a severe setback in his military operations when his ally, Emperor Otto IV of the Holy Roman Empire, was defeated by the French at the battle of Bouvines on 26 July. This ended any hope John may have harboured about recovering his lost territories in Europe. Adding to his worries was the Welsh problem, compounded by the fact that he was now faced with civil war from his own barons.

In the meantime, attacks against castles across Wales were still being maintained. In 1225 Laugharne castle was attacked and destroyed by Llywelyn who also attacked and destroyed Kidwelly castle. By now Llywelyn had an overwhelming following in the form of every great lord in Wales. They campaigned across the south of the country and either captured or destroyed many other great castles, including Llanstephan, Carmarthen, which was burnt after a siege lasting five days, Narberth, Cardigan and Cilgerran. In fact, so complete was their campaign that only Haverfordwest and Pembroke remained garrisoned for the king *(40)*.

In May 1215 King John was faced with a majority force of his barons who demanded he sign a treaty known as the Magna Carta. In essence the document declared that the Church could not be oppressed and that 'to no one will we sell, deny, or delay right or justice'. The king had to govern by its terms and could not himself be declared above the law. For the Welsh them-selves, this had a direct effect because those Welsh hostages had now to be released and the charters obtained by threats or intimidation from the Welsh rulers in 1211, had to be returned.

Llywelyn had supported the barons in their opposition of the king and their call for him to sign the Magna Carta. There now came several months of quiet in Wales and Llywelyn called for an assembly of Welsh rulers in early 1216, which was held at Aberdyfi. Here the reclaimed lands were divided among the Deheubarth rulers and all the lords paid homage to Llywelyn. It was obvious to all that Wales would be no place for a second powerful ruling figure and so it was that Gwenwynwyn was forced out of Powys into exile, and later died in England. Llywelyn was now the undisputed leader of the Welsh and he was openly referred to as 'Llywelyn Fawr', meaning 'Llywelyn the Great'. This title is believed to have been coined by the English chronicler Matthew Paris in his work *Chronica Majora*, after which it was widely used. In England however, Llywelyn was not viewed with the same reverence and was recognised as being the leader of the Welsh rather than a lord.

King John died on 18 October 1216, aged forty-nine years, leaving the throne to his son, who would rule as Henry III until 1272. But at the time of his accession Henry was only nine years old, and so it fell to William Marshall, earl of Pembroke, to act as his regent. The time was still very turbulent and it was not long before troubles once more started in Wales. In 1217 the Welsh resumed their attacks against castles and Llywelyn laid siege to Haverfordwest, one of the last remaining garrisons holding out for the king. It appears that it could never have been a serious siege because the Welsh forces withdrew when they were paid a bribe to depart. In 1220 Llywelyn returned to complete the task and destroy the castle. By that time, the Treaty of Lambeth, which had been signed in 1217 and effectively ended the Welsh wars and the civil war in England, was beginning to break down. Llywelyn had never been in agreement with the Treaty of Lambeth, he preferred instead the Peace of Worcester, which had been signed in 1218, because it confirmed all his terri-torial gains. For two years, following the Peace of Worcester, Llewelyn found himself at pains in attempting not to become totally alienated from England or antagonise the new king. After all, Henry was his brother-in-law and Llywelyn felt duty-bound to pay homage. Peace was across the land, but it was to be a short-lived respite from war.

HENRY III AND FURTHER WARS

Despite the best attempts to keep the peace, troubles and minor actions were fought during the early years of Henry III's reign *(41)*. Matters came to a head in 1224 when the king's regent Hubert de Burgh built a massive castle for the

41 King Henry III was only nine when he was proclaimed king. He would mount three campaigns into Wales, none of which produced any real results but which were financially crippling

king in Montgomery. William Marshall had died in 1219, having been the king's regent since 1216, and on his death Hubert de Burgh became the king's regent. Powerful and politically ambitious, Hubert also directed the young king in all aspects of politics. At the time of Hubert raising a new castle on behalf of his ward, Henry was sixteen years old. It would not be until 1227, when he was nineteen years old, that Henry would declare himself to be of age to rule without the direction of a guardian regent. In fact, by 1232 Hubert de Burgh would fall from favour, by which time Henry was sufficiently experienced in life at court.

However, all that was in the future. A campaign was launched into Wales under the guidance of Hubert de Burgh in 1223, the result of which was the new castle in Montgomery. He also captured Cardigan and Carmarthen, both of which would later serve as bases of operations from where campaigns could be mounted. This proved too much for the Welsh and in 1224 war erupted once again. Three more campaigns followed, the first of which was launched in 1228, only one year after Henry had begun to personally rule, and it petered out without achieving any real results. The second campaign was launched in 1231 and from writings in the Brut we learn the Welsh were using siege equipment at Cardigan:

> That same Maelgwn [Ieuanc] and Owain ap Gruffydd and their men, and with
> them the lord Lleywelyn's men, went for a second time to the town of
> Cardigan; and they laid siege to the castle. And after a few days they breached
> it with catapults, till the garrison was forced to surrender the castle and leave it.

The castle would again return to Norman control by 1240. The third
campaign in 1233 did not result in anything from which Henry could directly
benefit. Whilst visiting Grosmont castle during the last campaign, Henry had
come very close to being captured by Llywelyn. Using the classic Welsh tactic
of attacking by night, Llywelyn took the garrison by complete surprise, and
captured the castle. Fortunately for the king and his followers, they had set up
camp outside the castle walls, and were able to make good their escape, if
somewhat in haste, when the attack was made.

These were only the opening rounds in Henry's dealings with the Welsh
and later in his reign would he come to realise what adroit adversaries they
were. Following those actions, which were little more than probing engagements to test each other's state of preparedness, it would be the judicious
manoeuvrings on the part of Llywelyn who in 1234 brought into force the
Pact of Myddle that concluded a peace. There was sporadic fighting between
the Welsh rulers and in the fifty-six-year-long reign of Henry III the resistance
against England continued almost unabated. In fact, one is inclined to opine
that had the Welsh expended as much time and energy in combating the
Anglo-Normans as they did one another, there is every chance they would
have advanced their cause much further.

Llywelyn was shrewd enough to use marriage to secure his position. His
four daughters were married into Anglo-Norman marcher families and this
secured for him stability. His two sons were in fact half-brothers: Gruffydd was
the result of an earlier marriage and Dafydd ap Llywelyn was born to Joan,
which made him the nephew to Henry III. When it came to choosing a
successor there could be no contest for Dafydd had royal blood in his veins, no
matter how diluted. Llywelyn made a generous provision for Gruffydd, but the
choice of inheritance was not viewed as being fair and caused great divide
among the family. In 1238, Llywelyn planned to convene a gathering of Welsh
rulers at Strata Florida, possibly with the purpose of announcing his abdication
and for the rulers to pay homage to Dafydd. Henry learned of this and sent
word that they should not attend the meeting. The king was playing a
dangerous game in becoming involved with Welsh politics. In April 1240,
Llywelyn died and Dafydd inherited his father's position as ruler of Gwynedd.

Henry summoned Dafydd ap Llywelyn to meet him in Gloucester, where
he was knighted. But, in typical tradition there were clauses attached to the
bestowment as laid out in the Treaty of Gloucester. Under the terms laid out
in the treaty, in future all Welsh rulers had to pay homage to the king, which
Dafydd and all other rulers complied with. All of Llywelyn's lands were confis-

cated and the principality was broken up. It was a degrading moment for the proud rulers, in particular for Dafydd, who attempted to recover some standing and railed against the king. This angered Henry, and he invaded north Wales in a lightning campaign of 1241, which brought about Dafydd's surrender at Gwen Eigron. The campaign was concluded by the Treaty of Gwern Eigron which stripped away even more territory from Dafydd. He had to cede the *cantref* of Englefield to the crown and, if that was not enough, the Treaty of London laid out that should Dafydd die without heirs, all his lords would be forfeit to the crown also. To add to this humiliation Dafydd had to give over his half-brother Gruffydd, who would later be killed in 1244 as he attempted to escape from the Tower of London.

On learning of the death of Gruffydd, Dafydd was free to openly rebel against the king and regain his lost lands. In 1245 a campaign was launched against him from Chester, but it was doomed to collapse due to lack of provisions like other campaigns before it. Another campaign, led by Nicholas de Molis, was planned for the summer of 1246 and would be launched from Carmarthen. Events took an unexpected turn when Dafydd died very suddenly in February 1246. He left no heir and it looked as though his lands would pass to the crown. However, his half-brother, the recently killed Gruffydd, had had four sons: Owain, Llywelyn, Dafydd and Rhodri. Of these, Llywelyn was in Gwynedd at the time of his uncle's death, where he was providing him with support against the king. In the eyes of many this made him the natural successor. The eldest brother, Owain, disputed this and marched into Gwynedd, thereby entering into a family squabble which threatened to weaken them even further. Armies of the king were marching against them and to compound matters, a famine was devastating the country. In their weakened state, the two brothers were left with no alternative but to accept the terms of the Treaty of Woodstock on 30 April 1247, which stripped them of all their lands except for Gwynedd, west of the River Conwy.

Llywelyn was determined to fight back against the king and made an alliance by joining forces with Gruffudd ap Madog, the native lord of Bronfield. In 1251 Llywelyn and Owain enlisted the support of Maredudd ap Rhys Gryg of Dryslwyn and Rhys Fychan of Ystrad-Twyi, where castles had been built. Owain decided to change sides and allied himself with his brother Dafydd, and together they challenged Llywelyn. Now facing dissent from two of his own he was forced to fight them at the battle of Bryn Derwin in 1255. He defeated their army and was established as the ruler of Gwynedd. In victory he was magnanimous and spared their lives, choosing instead to imprison them. Dafydd was released the following year and joined his brother in fighting but Owain was to remain a prisoner for twenty-two years. With his affairs settled in his own principality Llywelyn was able to concentrate on the campaign which lay ahead. In November 1256, he crossed the River Conwy to give aid and support to the people of the four *cantrefs* who had appealed to him for help in relieving them from what they saw as the extortionate rule of royal officials.

The *cantrefs* in question lay in the area between the Rivers Conwy and Dee and in 1254 had been granted to Prince Edward, the eldest son of Henry III. This gift of all the king's lands in Wales was intended to not only provide the young prince with a source of income, but also to give him experience as a ruler, in anticipation of his succession to the full responsibilities of kingship. After a week of campaigning, the four *cantrefs*, apart from two castles, Diserth and Deganwy, had fallen to Llywelyn's forces. His successes continued for the next two years and he gained the lands of Meirionnydd, Deheubarth and Powys. In 1257, his Welsh forces defeated a royal army, led by Stephen Bauzan, in open battle at Cymerau near Llandeilo, but it was not exploited when the planned campaign into north Wales by the lords of Deheubarth collapsed. Henry led a campaign into Gwynedd but it was badly organised and never threatened Llywelyn's forces. By 1258, virtually every Welsh ruler, with the exception of Gruffydd ap Gwenwynwyn of southern Powys, were allied to Llywelyn's cause. Indeed, they paid homage to him and he was now openly calling himself the Prince of Wales.

In his book *The Thirteenth Century 1216–1307*, M. Powicke, states of Llywelyn's claim: 'His assumption of the title was more than a gesture, it was both the answer to a challenge and a declaration of purpose'. He was standing for Welsh rule and disputing ownership of the lands given to Prince Edward in 1254. All that was left now was for Llywelyn to make peace with Henry, which in 1259 he intended to do by making a payment of £16,500. Henry, beset with troubles both in England and in France, was in no position to argue or mount a campaign and settled instead for a truce, which brought about a temporary peace.

Fighting broke out in 1260 when Llywelyn attacked Builth and destroyed the castle, taking the lordship from Roger Mortimer. Two years later Mortimer was again attacked by Welsh forces, this time in his lordship Maelienydd, and the castle of Cefnllys was destroyed. The ease with which these castles appear to have been destroyed indicates that they were still of a very basic motte-and-bailey design, probably with earth-and-timber defences. In 1263 Llywelyn campaigned through Blaenllynfi and Brecon, before going on to capture the castles at Deganwy and Diserth between August and September that year. In the face of such an overwhelming force, Gruffydd ap Gwenwynwyn felt compelled to ally himself with Llywelyn and his younger brother Dafydd.

By 1263 the presence of England was so weakened that many rulers no longer regarded it as a serious threat to Wales. King Henry III was at this time facing a crisis in the form of a civil war in his own country as the barons, led by Simon de Montfort, revolted against the monarchy. It now appeared that the Welsh had an English ally for the first time as Llywelyn and Simon de Montfort openly supported one another. Their actions together resulted in the

42 Caerphilly castle built by Gilbert of Gloucester. It was protected by strong walls and an advanced system of water obstacles. Although damaged in early attacks by the Welsh it was completed to become a strong centre from which operations could be planned

Treaty of Pipton, in June 1265, whereby de Montfort, in the name of the king, recognised Llywelyn as the Prince of Wales and the overlord of other Welsh rulers. In return Llywelyn promised homage to Henry III and to make a payment of £20,000 over a ten-year period. Llywelyn had proven himself to be an astute military commander, who by judicious use of upland routes across the hills, could move his army from one end of the country to another in less time than any previous Welsh leader. He realised that to defeat his enemies, particularly the English, mobility was the key secret to any success. This fact he instilled into his army and they were stimulated to move at speed.

The deal brokered between Wales and England, as laid out in the Treaty of Pipton, was not legally binding, and Llywelyn, being equally aware of politics, as well as a master tactician, realised this. Two years later, with civil war in England at an end, Llywelyn was offered the Treaty of Montgomery on 29 September 1267. In this he was still recognised as the Prince of Wales and overlord. But, on this occasion, the court of Henry III was able to act without duress and the treaty was formally and legally recognised. Llywelyn would pay homage to the king and in turn would have homage paid to him by the Welsh lords. The terms of the treaty were agreed by the Welsh and English, and it appeared as though stability and peace were at last coming to the border between the two countries. Just as it seemed as if trade could once more be established and life return to some semblance of normality, Llywelyn attacked Caerphilly castle, on which building work had been started in January 1267 by Earl Gilbert of Gloucester, and damaged much of what had been built. Gilbert managed to fight back and by 1272 had reclaimed his castle, into the defences of which he was incorporating a sophisticated system of water obstacles. Caerphilly castle was massive with only two entrances, a large structure known as a hornwork and a central inner ward, it was a formidable castle by any standard *(42)*.

Llywelyn was now faced with the task of forging his newly won principality into a realm and ruling it as any other monarch. Given his new-found recognition as the Prince of Wales in accordance with the Treaty of Montgomery, Llywelyn considered himself to be in a strong enough position to establish new castles without the permission of the king. Indeed, Llywelyn would go on to raise several castles during his lifetime, but the castle he established at Dolforwyn was the only one built on an entirely new site, with foundations specially prepared for the purpose. The castle at Dolforwyn, near Abermule, is believed to have been started in 1273, by which time Henry III was dead. It was to prove a cause for concern, because in the area immediately around the castle a small town was established. The site was becoming more than just a military stronghold, Llywelyn was creating a new borough, which provided him with a source of income, and where he even held court. Adding to the apprehension caused by such a powerful Welsh stronghold was the fact that it lay uncomfortably close to the English stronghold of Montgomery, which had in turn been built to replace Hen Domen of 200 years earlier.

In 1272 Llywelyn had planned to pay homage to the king, but Henry III died, aged sixty-five years, before the Welsh leader could make preparations for his journey. This was an excuse for Llywelwyn to renege on his payments and finally stop payment altogether. Henry III was succeeded by his thirty-three-year-old son who would reign as Edward I. Although this direct succession was never in dispute, Edward was abroad in Sicily, where he was staying as a guest at the court of King Charles, when news of his father's death reached him in 1272. He had just returned from fighting in Palestine, where he had been wounded. Edward learned of his inheritance through messengers, but remained unperturbed and continued the process of making a leisurely return to England, no doubt using the time to fully recover from his wound received in the Crusades. In fact, it would not be until August 1274, some eighteen months after the death of his father, that Edward would once more set foot on the soil of England. When he arrived he was informed of developments along with news of events in Wales, which included the fact that Llywelyn had not paid his dues. In February 1274, while Edward was still absent, Dafydd and

43 King Edward I: a highly educated monarch, he would leave an indelible mark on Wales with his castle-building programme

Gruffydd plotted to kill their brother Llywelyn. Learning of this he moved to have them arrested, but they fled to England where they were given sanctuary in the name of the absent king.

When Llywelyn was summoned to attend the king's coronation he remained conspicuously absent. Further summons to pay homage to his new king were all met with excuses. He refused to meet Edward even when the king travelled to Chester, on the principle that he harboured his brothers who plotted to kill him. The new king was insulted and outraged by Llywelyn's behaviour. However, Llywelyn stated that if his brothers were handed over, he would pay homage and all the monies now long overdue. This was more than the king could bear and Edward allowed Dafydd and Gruffyd to raid into their brother's lands from bases in England. Finally he decided he had tolerated enough insults from Wales and on 12 November 1276 the king declared war.

EDWARD I AND THE MIGHTY CASTLES

Edward was a highly educated man, well travelled, popular and extremely brave *(43)*. After fighting in the Crusades he was making his way back to his kingdom by an overland route, which took him through several countries, where he was warmly received. As an experienced soldier, he had proved his worth on the battlefield many times during the Crusades and in the jousting yards. He was thirty-three years of age when he inherited the throne of England, along with the problems of kingship and the prospect of war with disquietened neighbouring states. In Edward's case he returned to a country faced by war with Scotland, Wales and France. As it transpired, it would be Wales that would present him with the most problems, as it took prior place among the triumvirate of potential enemy states.

During his journey homeward around 1273 Edward stayed as the guest of Count Philip of Savoy in his castle of St Georges d'Esperanche. It was here that he is believed to have been shown examples of the amazing and very advanced defensive designs of an architect known as Master James of St Georges, who had built the castle of St Georges, from which he is understood to have taken the second part of his name. Master James was a highly experienced castle builder, being responsible for the design of several other castles in Savoy, as well as overseeing their construction. Edward's travels had taken him to the Near East, North Africa and many parts of Europe, where he would have become familiar with a wide range of castle design. In his rank as a prince he would have been well placed to observe at first hand the requirements needed of a castle from both the defenders' and attackers' point of view. On being introduced to Master James, it must have been like meeting a kindred spirit for Edward. The king probably knew from the onset that he would be able to make good use of Master James's talents as a castle builder, particularly in north Wales.

We know that Master James was still working in Savoy in 1275, the year after Edward's coronation, but by early 1278 we learn he was in north Wales, where he was personally directing Edward's vast castle-building programme. At one point we learn that Master James was being paid by his new master at the rate of three shillings per day. In modern terms that would be in the order of £173 per day. It was the unique combination of Edward's great financial resources and Master James's building talents which would produce a powerful group of castles in north Wales, which became referred to as 'the ring of iron'. During his long reign Henry III had spent large amounts on the repair, maintenance and improvement of existing castles, which somewhat limited the finances left for the building of new ones. But the partnership of Edward and Master James would produce a series of castles the like of which had never been seen anywhere in Europe at the time.

Together the two men planned a series of new castles in north Wales, through which Edward would be able to exert his domination of the country. The sites chosen for the new castles included, Flint, Rhuddlan, Aberystwyth, Ruthin, Conwy, Caernarfon, Harlech, Beaumaris on Anglesey, Builth and Hope. At some of these locations there had already existed castles but the extent of their rebuilding gave them the appearance of being new castles. These new royal castles were not the only fortifications to be raised at this time. Four other locations, Hawarden, Chirk, Denbigh and Holt, whilst not strictly speaking 'royal' castles were nevertheless very much a part of Edward's Welsh containment policy and could easily be incorporated into the rest of the castle-building programme. In fact, to give an idea of how both sets of castles could be used in conjunction with one another, between them the garrisons at Ruthin, Rhuddlan, Flint, Chester and Hawarden formed a 'great fortified triangle' which could be used to contain a Welsh uprising. These were termed as 'lordship' castles, which were licensed to be built by men whom Edward could trust and he rewarded them with large estates of land. For example, the lordship of Hawarden was granted to Roger de Clifford in 1281, where a motte-and-bailey structure had once stood before being destroyed by Llywelyn in 1265. In the war of 1282 it would again be one of the first castles to be attacked, probably because it was still in a state of construction and therefore very weak and open to attack. It was the revenues from these lands which funded the building of the castles and although the king had not paid for them, we can tell from their design that they were built to specifications laid out by Master James.

The building programme of these new castles was started around 1277 and for over twenty-five years proceeded on seventeen sites. At least fourteen were new, or virtually new, castles, with a number of Welsh castles being redesigned for use by the crown. In addition the border fortresses at Chester, Shrewsbury, Oswestry and Montgomery were strengthened. Under King Edward the country must have appeared as one giant building site, with labourers coming from all over England, not to mention the transport of materials to the separate sites. For example, in 1296 at the site of Caernarfon we learn there were about 400 skilled masons continuously at work and more than 1,000 labourers to mix the mortar and lime. In addition there were 200 carters, thirty smiths and carpenters, and a military guard of thirty men. The massive stone blocks were transported to the site by sea routes, for which a fleet of thirty boats were used, and 160 wagons moved the building material over land. This was being repeated across Wales at large sites such as Beaumaris, Harlech, Conwy and Rhuddlan. The whole enterprise cost Edward £80,000, which is in the order of some £40,000,000 by today's rates, and very nearly bankrupted one of the wealthiest nations in Europe at that time. The building work at the sites continued until the time of Edward's death in 1307, and even then not all the castles were complete. Flint was completed in 1280, but at Beaumaris castle the site was not ready to receive a garrison until 1298 and Caernarfon could not accept its garrison until 1299.

At the time of their being built these castles became the focus of great resentment, and were attacked at various times during the stages of building. For example, in 1282 Flint was attacked and besieged by Llywelyn Fawr, but

44 *Opposite* Hourding or bratticing, seen here recreated at Caerphilly castle. These wooden structures were used by the defenders of some Welsh castles. They allowed the defenders to engage attackers at the base of the castle walls

45 *Right* Recreated hourding or bratticing seen here at Caerphilly castle

the site was not captured. It is recorded how at the time of the attack the castle was fitted with the wooden hourding or bratticing which allowed the defenders to direct missiles at the base of the walls *(44 & 45)*. Later actions against Edward's castles included attacks directed towards Caernarfon in 1294 by Prince Madoc ap Llywelyn. At this action he set fire to some buildings and destroyed some of the building work, but the castle itself was not destroyed. Madoc also attacked Harlech in the same year without result, but at Conwy castle he gave cause for concern when the king was one of those trapped by the besieging force. Prince Madoc was pressing in on the defences and it was only the timely arrival of the fleet which rescued Edward. The defences of these great castles, such as at Harlech, Conwy and Caernarfon were inherently strong and so well laid out that they only required garrisons of between thirty and sixty men for their defence. Obviously they could accommodate greater numbers, but in the event they could be held by a small force of defenders until reinforcements arrived.

Another feature about the ring of great castles being raised was their strategic positioning, which offered mutual support. They were built at locations so that one was no more than one day's march from the next in the system. Thus, Flint could send reinforcements to aid Conwy, some 30 miles to the west, and, if required, Caernarfon could do the same. In the time that Master James was working on this great project for Edward I he lived in Wales and came to understand the people. Although a military architect, he understood military operations and tactics, and is believed at one time to have held Harlech castle for the king. In his position of authority and special relationship with the king he could correspond directly with Edward. In one such letter from James to Edward we learn of his assessment regarding the Welsh in the late thirteenth century when he wrote: 'You know that Welshmen will be Welshmen even if they appear to be pacified.' In other words, do not underestimate them for they will always come back to fight again.

THE WAR OF 1277

Edward had an astute military mind and his campaign into Wales was well organised both tactically and logistically. He was determined not to fail where previous kings had. He decided that the time had come for decisive action against Llywelyn and meticulous preparations were made for a campaign in north Wales during 1277. Firstly, the campaign would not advance along one main route; Edward planned to advance into Wales along three separate lines. That way he would split Welsh forces and overwhelm them by sheer numbers and aggressive action. His rear areas, from where he could expect reinforcements and supplies, were secure and would never be threatened. Furthermore, he had a fleet of ships which could sail up the coast to land troops or supplies. Never before had a campaign into Wales been so well prepared.

The three military commands advanced into Wales along lines which penetrated deeply into the country. In the north the command of Chester moved to defeat the lords of northern Powys and followed the coast along through Rhuddlan and Deganwy and pushed into Gwynedd. The Welsh could not hold the army and they burnt the castle at Dinas Bran to prevent its capture. Marching into Wales from Shrewsbury in the east, the king's army moved on to Montgomery and laid siege to Llywelyn's castle at Dolforwyn, deep in the Severn valley. Under the direction of Roger de Mortimer and the earl of Lincoln the besiegers took up positions on 31 March. They maintained pressure on the garrison and managed to reduce the water supply to the castle. On 8 April after an action lasting eight days, the castle at Dolforwyn surrendered. The besiegers had not had to attack the castle in frontal assault and their tactic of depriving the garrison of water had brought about a quick result. One part of the advancing column headed north through Powys Wenwynwyn and moved towards Gwynedd. The third advance was made from Carmarthen towards Dryslwyn and Dinefor, which was quickly taken with the support of Rhys ap Maredudd, lord of Dryslwyn. One column of the army turned eastwards and headed towards the castle at Carreg Cennen *(46)*. This site was

46 Carreg Cennen castle, a stone-built castle, was erected by the Welsh in a well-sited location, taking advantage of natural features including sheer drops into the river. The castle was attacked by forces of Edward I and the site captured

very strongly built with the southern flank of the castle overlooking a sheer drop into the river, and from which direction no attack could be launched. The other sides leading up to the castle are steeply sloping and the walls stoutly built. Despite this, the castle was taken by the king's army.

Llywelyn was hard pressed in the north and his brother, Dafydd, moved south to try and recruit support for the cause. He managed to gain Llandovery for a short time and also captured Llanbarden on 9 April. He was attacked by the king's forces shortly after and again in June. The Welsh managed to hold on and even raise support against the attacking English. Dafydd withdrew to the north leaving the local force to hold down the king's troops, which fell back on Cardigan and Carmarthen, where they regrouped in readiness for the next part of the campaign. This show of strength had not stopped the English, merely slowed down the advance. The king was cautious and knew he could take his time and advance only when he was ready. His forces were moved forwards and by July Gwynedd had been captured. The lords of Deheubarth were surrendering and Rhys ap Maredudd was taking the castles in the Tywi valley for the king.

King Edward was campaigning with his forces in the north, which were operating from Chester. In August his army comprised over 16,400 men. Of these some 7,000 were Welshmen, from whom the force of 1,000 archers was probably formed. Making up another part of his formidable army was a force of about 800 knights which were the elite of his fighting force. Along his route Edward established castles such as Flint and Ruddlan. He captured the ports on Anglesey so that his fleet could sail to his support whilst denying the Welsh any outside assistance. In the face of such a powerful force Llywelyn could offer little in the way of organised resistance and was forced to retreat into the mountain mass of Snowdonia. He probably felt that he could remain there in safety until he was ready to launch an attack. But he reckoned without Edward's determination. Llywelyn was isolated and with all the exits from Snowdonia blocked and communication with Anglesey, the source of his food supply, cut off his position was never going to improve. With his forces now facing starvation Llywelyn realised he had no other choice but to surrender. In November he emerged to accept the terms of the Treaty of Conwy. The terms were nominally severe, including heavy fines and lands being stripped from Llywelyn and hostages being exchanged. But Edward was magnanimous and did not enforce these terms to the letter. At Christmas Llywelyn attended court at Westminster and made his long-delayed homage to the king. The campaign had taken little under one year and there was peace again in North Wales, at least for the moment.

During the war of 1277 the Welsh had used traditional guerrilla warfare tactics, which for the first time had failed. Edward's army was highly experienced and the fact he also used a large number of Welshmen in his pay, probably meant they knew what to expect and how to protect themselves from the tactics of their countrymen. In the meantime, castle-building was being increased across the whole of Wales and repairs were being effected at those sites considered important to the crown's efforts at maintaining control. In October 1279, for example, at Aberystwyth castle we learn that a labour force was engaged in preparing the defences of the castle and town, the force including 176 masons, fourteen carpenters, five smiths, two plumbers and over 1,100 labourers. At exactly the same time as this was going on the great castles in the north were being planned. Also at Carmarthen in the same year Edward created an administrative centre to establish the town as a focal point of great importance.

The king was installing his nobles to act as royal officials across Wales and this angered many of the local lords, including Dafydd, who in March 1282 convinced his brother Llywelyn to once again rise in revolt against the English. This new rising by the Welsh was as sudden as it was unexpected and moved so quickly it caught the king unaware. On 21 March the forces of Llywelyn ap Gruffydd, led by his brother Dafydd, attacked Hawarden castle at night in March 1282 they captured it with such speed and guile that they seized the constable of the castle, Roger de Clifford, while he was still in bed. To be fair, however, the castle was in a state of construction and so would have presented an easy target to attack; equally in fairness, the garrison would in all probability have been a small or token force with only workmen to make up the numbers. This was followed by a swift attack against Oswestry on 22 March and the castles at Aberystwyth, Llandovery and Carreg Cennan. The repercussions of this and other manoeuvrings by the Welsh were taken very seriously by King Edward, who responded by hurling the might of the English army against the country.

Edward was coming under increasing pressure from various parties to support a number of enterprises, including a request from the Pope that he serve on a Crusade. He was in no mood to mediate and he ordered his armies to once more advance into Wales from Chester, Montgomery and Carmarthen. Llywelyn was again pushed back into Snowdonia and just as defeat appeared to be imminent he managed to break out and head south towards Builth. It was here on 11 December that he was engaged in battle by the Marcher Lord Roger Lestrange at Orewin Bridge (sometimes written as Irfon Bridge). Llywelyn was almost certainly killed by Stephen de Frankton of Shropshire, after which he was decapitated and his head displayed before the victorious English troops. Roger Lestrange wrote to King Edward and informed him of the victory over the Welsh:

> Inform the king that the troops under Roger's command fought with Llywelyn ap Gruffydd in the land of Buellt [Builth] on Friday next after the feast of St Nicholas, that llywelyn ap Gruffydd is dead, his army defeated, and all the flower of his army dead, as the bearer of this letter will tell.

The Welsh mourned his loss and referred to him as '*Ein Elyw Olaf*' ('Our last great leader').

However, that still left Dyfed to campaign. He used the site of Castell y Bere, deep in the Dysynni valley, as his base of operations. This was a castle built by Llywelyn ap Iowerth around 1221. It was very strongly built and located in a remote part of the Cadair Idris Range. During January and February 1283, Edward advanced with great caution and by March had established himself at Aberconwy in Gwynedd. From here the king maintained his operations against the garrison at Castell y Bere until they finally surrendered on 25 April. He had captured Dolwyddlan castle and with his other castles he was in a strong position. Dafydd had escaped from Castell y Bere to continue fighting, but support was waning and he was growing weaker by the day. He was captured in June 1283 near to the site of Aber, the Welsh royal palace. It is believed he was seized by some of his own countrymen and handed over to the king's forces. Dafydd was taken to Shrewsbury where he was hung, drawn and quartered, a most horrible form of execution. With the deaths of these two leaders it would have appeared that all threats of uprisings had been removed.

There were many Welsh leaders but only a few of them rose to actual prominence. That is not to say that those who did not rise to greatness as military campaigners resisted any less than those who did conduct wars against the English. For those Welshmen who chose to resist did so in whatever way they could, be it militarily or refusing service in a royal household. This refusal to be subjugated was something which baffled all who invaded the country. Certainly by the thirteenth century many Welshmen were serving in the army of the king and also as mercenaries on the Continent. It was their experience in battle which they brought back with them that proved invaluable when campaigning against the English and besieging castles. In 1287 there was yet another rebellion in Wales, this time by a local lord who had at one time had been loyal to Edward, but had become disaffected by broken promises from the crown. Rhys ap Maredudd of Dryslwyn was a member of the Deheubarth rulers and had supported the king against Llywelyn in 1282, for which services he had been promised many things. One of these promises had been the lordship of Dinefwr castle. When this was not forthcoming Rhys ap Maredudd rose in rebellion against his former masters. The king was not in England at the time, but even if he had been, it is likely that the campaign would have been conducted all the same.

This latest in a long line of Welsh rebellions was a serious matter and Rhys raised a powerful army. He began his campaign on 8 June 1287 and several castles quickly fell to him, including Dinefwr, Carreg Cennan, Llandovery, Swansea, Aberystwyth and Brecon. Although the king was absent he was kept informed of developments and he dispatched a letter to the knights in the districts of Salop and Stafford in which he ordered them: 'to assist with their horses, arms and power Roger Lestrange, whom the king is sending to Wales to repress the rebellion of Rhys son of Mereduc and his accomplices of Welshmen.'

Rhys had established a garrison at Dryslwyn castle, set high on a steep hill overlooking the River Tywi. Although in a strong position and a commanding vantage point, its elevation actually worked against its own defences because it could easily be surrounded and cut off from any relief force. Towards the end of June that is exactly the position in which Rhys discovered himself. The origin of the castle is unclear, but it is understood to have been built by Rhys Gryg on a site that may have been formerly occupied by earlier castles. The forces ranged against Rhys ap Maredudd were considerable and included heavy siege equipment capable of hurling massive stones to batter the walls. Conducting the siege was Earl Edmund of Cornwall, King Edward's brother, who had a force of over 11,000 men under his immediate command, including 600 horsemen. The Marcher Lords, whom Edward had extolled to give support, provided a further 12,500 men to suppress this rebellion.

The siege of Dryslwyn castle would last several weeks and see all forms of siege warfare being used in attempts to reduce the garrison. One item known to have been specially brought to the site was a huge device known as a trebuchet, which was a massive catapult constructed from wood, some examples of which could hurl stone projectiles over 500 yards *(47)*. The trebuchet was an expensive and complicated weapon and was the heavyweight in the arsenal of siege equipment which could be brought to bear against castles *(48)*. Probably invented around 1250, it operated on the counterpoise system, which is to say a heavily weighted box was used to power the throwing arm. The operators, referred to as *gynours*, pulled the throwing arm down, elevating the weighted box. It was held in this position by a simple release mechanism while it was loaded with a stone. When ready the arm was released and the projectile was launched. It was not accurate but it could pound away at castle walls and even be used to propel clay pots filled with quicklime which would break on impact and blind the garrison. The trebuchet was also powerful enough to throw a dead and diseased animal carcass into the castle in an attempt to try and spread disease among the garrison. A trebuchet fitted with a throwing arm of 50ft in length and powered by a counterpoise weight of 20,000lbs would propel a stone weighing 300lbs out to a distance of over 300ft *(49)*.

We do not know the exact dimensions of the trebuchet used at the siege of Dryslwyn but it must have been impressive. According to chronicles of the period it required forty oxen to pull it over smooth ground and sixty oxen to pull it over uneven ground. It was considered important enough to warrant its own guard to protect it against attack, and this comprised twenty horsemen and almost 500 men-at-arms. A team of twenty masons was continuously employed in preparing the stone projectiles for its use. In total just fewer than 500 such projectiles were prepared for the trebuchet at Dryslwyn. The bill for preparing it for use at the siege came to £14 (£7,000 by modern standards) which included the purchase of ropes, timber and metal fittings. In addition to this the besiegers also had smaller catapults throwing lighter stone projectiles weighing between 10lbs and 50lbs, which would have had ranges of between 350 yards and 500 yards. These would have harassed the garrison and produced some localised damage.

As well as being cut off from any relief force the castle was also subjected to mining operations whilst also being bombarded by the stone projectiles of the catapults and trebuchet. Digging tunnels, or mining, under the walls of castles had been used successfully at other sieges where it had led to the collapse of the walls. The technique was relatively straightforward and required men to simply dig a tunnel under the walls of the castle. The excavation was supported by beams to prevent premature collapse and a fire was set at the appropriate moment to burn the beams away. This weakened the foundations of the walls, which collapsed under their own weight. The walls at Dryslwyn castle were

47 Above left A recreated trebuchet catapult siege engine. It had immense power and some designs could hurl heavy stone projectiles considerable distances with great striking force. This model at Caerphilly castle is being readied for operation

48 Above right A recreated trebuchet catapult siege engine. It is seen here being readied for operation at Caerphilly castle

49 Left A detail of a recreated trebuchet catapult siege engine. It is seen here being readied for operation at Caerphilly castle

mined between 20 and 30 August but the tunnel collapsed killing 150 men, including William de Montchensy.

Sensing that all was now lost, Rhys abandoned the castle and fled. The besiegers had achieved their aim and captured the castle using the most advanced methods known to them at the time. Rhys moved to Newcastle Emlyn where he was followed in November. In January 1288, Edward returned to the country and made his way to the castle where Rhys was resisting. The full range of siege equipment was once more ranged against the garrison and the castle captured. Rhys once again managed to escape, but on this occasion he became a fugitive from the king's forces. He would remain a wanted man until he was finally captured in 1292. Rhys had never been a popular man among other Welsh leaders and when he was hanged at York for his actions against the king there were few who mourned his execution.

The closing years of the thirteenth century in Wales were far from peaceful and King Edward was faced with more rebellions and attacks on his castles. In September 1294 Madog ap Llywelyn, a younger son in one of the ruling families in Gwynedd, had been trying unsuccessfully to recover lost lands through means of the court. Deeply frustrated, he rebelled against the king. He enjoyed some support for his cause, including Morgan ap Maredudd in the south-east. Like Rhys only six years before, he managed to catch the royal officials unawares. His early strikes were swift and produced results. He attacked and defeated the earl of Lincoln in battle at Denbigh and managed to ambush and kill the deputy-justiciar of south Wales *(50)*. His forces moved on to burn Llan-faes and capture Caernarfon. Madog invaded Anglesey, where he hanged the royal sheriff, Roger de Pulesden, a personal friend of King Edward. Edward was set to depart for a campaign in France when he heard the news from Wales. He hastened to the country and took up residence in Conwy castle *(51)*. Madog invested the castle and the besiegers were threatening its security. It was the timely intervention of the king's fleet which rescued him. During the winter of 1294–1295, the English fought back and went on the offensive, seizing back Anglesey and defeating Madog in battle at Maes Moydog in Powys. Edward ordered a castle to be raised on the island to prevent any such further incident. Work was started on Beaumaris castle and by the autumn of 1295 over £6,000 had been spent on the site. It was ready to accept its first garrison by 1298, which comprised ten men-at-arms, twenty bowmen and 100 foot soldiers. Madog was captured and imprisoned in the Tower of London for the rest of his life. This had been another short, but bitter campaign for the king. Such actions were costing him greatly in financial terms, apart from the cost of building his new castles. It is estimated that Madog's rebellion cost the crown an estimated £55,000 (approximately £27,500,000 in modern terms) to suppress. No wonder, then, coming on top of the cost of building his new castles, that the country was facing economic ruin.

50 Above Denbigh castle, built by Hugh de Lacy in 1282, was captured by the Welsh in 1294. The castle was not completed until 1311, after the death of de Lacy

51 Opposite above Conwy castle and its massive imposing walls, built to the advanced design laid out by Master James of St Georges

52 Opposite below Caernarfon castle with its towering defences and strategic site overlooking the southern end of the Menai Straits between mainland Wales and the Isle of Angelsey. It commanded the surrounding region and was only one day's march away from the next castle in the chain.

The rising of 1294–1295 had caught the English off guard, but the new castles, it was hoped, would prevent this from happening again. By now the two countries had been fighting for almost 250 years and a settlement was far from being in sight. The fighting had not been on a constant basis, but it would have been enough of a drain on resources by a country which refused to be subdued. Edward at this point in his reign and with more than enough experience of the Welsh, was beginning to listen to what they had to say. He understood their grievances and took steps to bring some compromise to the situation in an attempt to prevent the outbreak of war. Edward on the other hand was harsh in his treatment of the Scots. Indeed, not without good reason that was he known as 'The Hammer of the Scots', and he repressed them fiercely. Transgressions by the Marcher Lords were punished, not because they had made war in Wales, but because they had disobeyed his order not to fight.

In 1301 King Edward conferred on his eldest surviving son, also called Edward, the title of Prince of Wales. Prince Edward was born at Caernarfon castle in April 1284, and at the time of his presentation to the Welsh people he was only seven years old *(52)*. Tradition has it that the ceremony took place at Caernarfon castle, but it is more than likely that the event occurred at Rhuddlan, which was a much older, established castle. King Edward made the gesture as some move towards recompense for the way in which he had dealt with the Welsh. His actions could be viewed as too little too late, for the damage had already been done and people have long memories. The last years of his reign and life were relatively quiet with regards to events in Wales. Edward died in 1307, in his sixty-eighth year. In his life he had been a strong and powerful king, full of energy and resourcefulness. His son and heir, who would rule as Edward II, would not have the same traits as his father, but like his father, this king too would have his share of dealings with Wales and the Welsh people.

1 Previous page   The Henry VII Tower in Pembroke castle where Henry Tudor, King Henry VII, was born in 1457. The dynasty he founded in 1485 lasted 116 years and the castle has become synonymous with the Tudors

2 Top   The magnificent Caerphilly castle with its 'leaning' tower, which is the result of slighting during the Civil War. It is reputed to have a greater degree of incline than the world-famous Leaning Tower of Pisa in Italy

3 Above   Monmouth castle, where King Henry V was born in 1387. Not much is now left of this once impressive site

4 Top Caernarfon castle, one of the massively strong fortifications built during the reign of Edward I and intended to bring control over north Wales

5 Above Conwy castle, quietly imposing and deceptive strong. Another of Edward I's inherently strong castles in north Wales

6   Cardiff castle, evolved from the wooden walled, motte-and-bailey style ordered to be built by William I in 1081. The shell keep on its mound would have dominated the entire area during the Middle Ages

7   Coity castle was Norman in style but over the centuries was altered to keep pace with changes in military style. It was besieged by the forces of Owain Glyn Dwr, and today is largely in decay, but still impressive

8   Rhuddin is one of the castles built for Edward I by Master James after 1277. It was capable of being supplied by sea and even had a small quay built within its outer defences where a ship could moor and unload its cargo. The four 'drum' towers gave all-round defence to the site

9   The uncompleted Beaumaris castle, which covered the western side of the Menai Straits on the Isle of Anglesey. It formed part of the 'ring of iron' established for Edward I in order to control northern Wales

10 *Above*   The very strong gatehouse of Beaumaris castle on the Isle of Anglesey. Very low in silhouette, it also had defensive positions built into the walls from where artillery could be fired

11 *Left*   Llawhaden castle, although never attacked seriously, in the sixteenth century Thomas Wyriott did attack it to rescue Lady Tanglost, who had been imprisoned there on the charge of witchcraft. An earlier castle on the site had been destroyed in 1193 by Lord Rhys

12 Above Coity castle was subjected to a siege by Owain Glyn Dwr's forces and over the later years became a Tudor home. It was subject to much remodelling and changed ownership several times

13 Below Built around 1110 by Gerald of Windsor, Cilgerran withstood many attacks. In 1405 it fell to the forces of Owain Glyn Dwr. In 1414 it was granted to the duke of Gloucester, brother of Henry V. After 1485, Henry VII granted it to the Vaughan family, who lived in the castle until the Civil War

14 Above The interior of the shell keep at Cardiff castle, showing the quite spacious area within which living quarters and food-preparation areas would have been located

15 Left Re-enactor showing how provisions could be moved using a reconstructed winch and wicker basket, very much in the manner of the medieval period

16 Above left   Sir Miles Picard, a retainer of
Bernard Neufmarche, built the first motte-and-
bailey castle at Tretower. It evolved into a shell
keep and later a manor house was built in the
vicinity of the castle

17 Above right   The gatehouse at Harlech castle,
one of the great castles built by Edward I. The
most impressive part of any castle, the gatehouse,
is also the strongest point. This is no exception
and is still awe-inspiring

18 Right   The massive Queen's Gate at
Caernarfon castle. At such an elevation it was
difficult to attack directly and the access was fitted
with a specially designed 'turning bridge'. The
arch above also incorporates 'murder holes' from
where projectiles could be dropped on attackers

19 Above   Carew castle developed from a motte–and–bailey design and was built by Gerald of Windsor in 1105. Over the centuries it developed into a Tudor mansion but its importance as a defensive site never diminished. It was attacked by Parliamentarian forces in 1645 and much damage inflicted during the fighting

20 Left   Kidwelly Castle with its 'walls within walls' construction made it inherently strong and was based on a feature copied from strongholds encountered in the Middle East during the Crusades

21 Opposite   The great tower at Pembroke castle which is 75ft high and is still roofed. The thickened base protected it from undermining and artillery fire. It provides a commanding view of the surrounding area

22 Opposite Drysllwyn castle, showing the commanding position and thickness of walls

23 Right The well at Denbigh castle. A secure water supply was essential for the survival of any castle when under attack

24 Below The gatehouse at Manorbier castle

25 The curtain walls of Beaumaris castle seen from the inside. They are low-lying and extremely stout, allowing them to withstand artillery

26 The inner walls of Beaumaris castle, of the 'walls within walls' design. Although never fully completed, the site represents great strength

27 Above left The one-time access from the River Rhuddlan along which ships could navigate to supply Rhuddlan castle directly

28 Above right The stout walls and towers as designed by Master James, the architect for Edward I

29 Right A view from the walls of Coity castle showing the outer earthworks built to extend the castle's defences

30 Overleaf The gatehouse at Llawhaden castle, which although never directly involved in outright war, was an important centre of power for the Church in Wales

4

THE FOURTEENTH CENTURY

At the start of the fourteenth century Edward I still ruled the country very firmly. He had learned great lessons in how best to deal with the Welsh and had come to terms with his treatment of them. In fact, one is almost inclined to say that in his later life he had developed an attachment to the people. After all, he had presented his son Edward, to the Welsh as the Prince of Wales. By this stage the lineage of the monarchy was such that it could no longer be regarded as being Norman, but instead more as English. These were the Plantagenet monarchs and although descended from the Normans they were now very distinct from the French monarchs of the time.

It is possible that the beginning of this affinity between the crown and the Welsh people could be traced back to 1277 when Edward is known to have had some 9,000 Welsh infantry in his army at Chester for his campaign. At this early stage in his reign it is unlikely that he would have had the same regard for the fighting prowess of the Welsh that he would have, say, twenty years later. It would be fair to say that Edward and other English military leaders at the time realised the fighting value of Welshmen, which accounts for the relatively high proportion in the English army at this time. Doubtless not all Welshmen in the army of Edward I were wholly loyal to him. Rather they were merely seeking wages which could be used to support their families back home. Also, by serving the king, their home communities were less likely to be persecuted by the English.

In the closing years of the thirteenth century the English came to recognise the potential contained in a new weapon developed in south Wales, especially in the area of Gwent. This was the longbow, and the Welsh archers who used it would gain the respect and fear of ally and enemy alike. As early as 1282 the majority of Edward's forces were archers and during the Hundred Years War the reliance on these men as a shock force would wreak havoc on the French. Indeed, the archers from Crickhowell, where a castle had been built, were highly regarded for their skills.

53 Re-enactor showing how a medieval archer looked. Archers would become increasingly important troops on the battlefield and at the sites of sieges where they could shoot directly at strategic targets. Note the bracer on his left arm to protect it from the enormous impact of the bowstring on releasing the arrow

As the Welsh had learned lessons in warfare from their battles against the Normans, so now began the English to learn from the Welsh. In his book *English Military Institutions on the Welsh Marches*, F. Suppe states: 'English military institutions were improved by borrowing from the Welsh practice and modifications made to meet the challenges posed by the Welsh'. It is said that imitation is the sincerest form of flattery, and in warfare this does not come any higher.

It was obvious that if one could harness this nascent force which promised such enormous power on the battlefield, it would surely be better to have them as allies than be faced by their deadly hail of arrows *(53)*. This is exactly what would come to happen and during the Hundred Years War, which started in 1337, time after time the Welsh archers would decimate the ranks of the French nobility which formed their knightly class.

KING EDWARD II: 1307–1327

When Edward I died in 1307 his son was proclaimed king and would rule as Edward II. The old king had been strong and whilst Edward ascended the throne at the age of twenty-three, he was not wise in the ways of ruling. He

54 The ill-fated King Edward II, who proved to be a weak and foolish ruler. He was feckless during his reign despite being popular in Wales. Ultimately he was murdered in a most despicable manner, but even in death the Welsh still held him in high esteem

was sympathetic towards the Welsh and concerned over their genuine grievances, but he would not prove to be a strong-willed or forceful king. Indeed, during his reign of twenty years Edward II would be faced with frequent internal bickerings, civil war, being cuckolded by his wife and political disobedience, all before finally being captured, imprisoned and murdered.

Edward II took to the Welsh personally and they responded in kind by supporting him through all the troubles which beset his reign *(54)*. This was a continuation of loyalty which had really started during the reign of Edward I, when the king had shown great faith and trust in the Welsh as fighting troops. At the battle of Falkirk, 22 July 1298, Edward had an army of some 18,500 to face a Scottish army of 10,200 under Sir William Wallace. Edward's force comprised about 12,500 infantry, of which 10,500 were from Wales. At least a full third of the horses used by his cavalry were bred in Wales. This battle would come to be seen as marking a trust, an almost inter-dependability, between the king and the Welsh. At the battle of Falkirk the Welsh archers, drawn mainly from Glamorgan, gave the king a resounding victory. The Scots lost more than half their total forces, whilst the king's army suffered only 200 killed from his cavalry force. The threat from Scotland was all but over and the Welsh had been instrumental in defeating the king's enemy.

Only three years earlier, in 1295, the English and Welsh had been fighting one another equally fiercely, if not perhaps on the same scale. However, Edward I had become chastened in his attitude towards the Welsh and this understanding would continue to be fostered by Edward II, who would retain large numbers of Welshmen, especially archers, in his army. Indeed, Edward would have known all about his father's victory at Falkirk and would have been anxious to emulate his father in his own campaigns. In his book, *A History of Wales*, the eminent Welsh historian John Davies states:

> The few pence a day earned by the soldiers were important to the Welsh economy; the many wanderings of the Welsh recruits enriched the culture of Wales and their valour gave rise to new tales of heroism.

This of course is perfectly correct in every form. The trend to use Welshmen in the English army was maintained by Edward II, and the survivors of foreign wars and battles had experience which would prove invaluable in training new recruits and engendering reliability in battle. For example, Edward II would have 'inherited' into his army some of the survivors of the 5,300 Welshmen who had served in his father's campaign in Flanders in 1297. From them he could build up a seasoned force with high morale and steady nerves in battle.

There were occasions when it was due to the steadfastness of such troops that total disaster was narrowly averted. Such an event happened when Edward II invaded Scotland in 1314 and met armies of a different calibre to those encountered by his father sixteen years earlier. On 24 June 1314, the army of Edward II met the Scottish army of Robert the Bruce at Bannockburn. Edward had an army estimated at 60,000, comprising 5,000 heavy cavalry, 10,000 light cavalry, 20,000 archers and 25,000 infantry. There were approximately 5,000 Welshmen in his infantry force alone and a high proportion of his horses were bred in Wales. The Scottish army had a strength of 41,500 of whom 1,500 were heavy cavalry. On the face of it, the English army with its numerical superiority would appear to have had the advantage.

However, appearances can be deceiving and the battle went badly for the English. The strong force of Welsh and English archers were sited poorly on the battlefield and they were not able to bring the full weight of their striking power to bear on the Scottish forces. The Scots pressed home their attack and the English army began to collapse. Some sources say that Edward panicked and fled the battlefield which in turn signalled his army to turn and run in a wholesale and disorganised retreat from the advancing Scottish army. The Scots pursued them and cut down thousands in their bid to escape. The battle had cost the Scots 4,000 killed and Edward had lost 15,000 valuable men. The king had to abandon any thought about invading Scotland, unlike his father who had the epithet 'Hammer of the Scots'. Edward II had to strengthen the garrisons of those castles in Wales, particularly in the north of the country and along the coastal regions because a Scottish invasion was greatly feared. The threat would not diminish until around 1388. Had the archers at Bannockburn been better deployed they could have cut the Scottish army to shreds at ranges of around 250 yards. As it was they could only do their best from where they were positioned on the battlefield and give support to the troops as they fled the deadly Scots. The English losses had been high, but they could have been greater had not some groups fought on to protect the withdrawal from the battlefield. Bannockburn was an experience which the king would never forget and neither would those ordinary soldiers who had been there.

CIVIL WAR

In the meantime it had by no means been peaceful in Wales during the first years of the reign of Edward II. The large-scale battles, besieging of castles and rebellions appeared to be at an end, to be replaced instead by devious means more akin to political machinations, rather than fighting and not always necessarily involving the Welsh themselves. In 1309, only two years into his rule, Edward was faced by a power struggle in Wales which began when the last of the native lords of Powys died. This was compounded five years later when the earl of Gloucester was killed at Bannockburn in 1314, along with Gilbert de Clare, lord of Glamorgan. Neither of these powerful figures had heirs, which left their possessions open to seizure and only added further to those problems fermenting in Wales.

The vacant lordship was seized on by Hugh Despenser, a favourite of the king. To outsiders this move was not viewed well, because Despenser already had extensive lands in Wales, including castles, and this increase in his possessions only served to widen the divide and cause much resentment. In 1321 the voices of disapproval finally erupted into war and the Despensers were defeated and sent into exile. Ever since the beginning of his reign, Edward had never been fully settled with his barons and lords, and in 1322 he finally declared war on them, attacking among others, Thomas, earl of Lancaster. The fact that he was the king's cousin did not protect him and when he was defeated in battle at Boroughbridge in 1322 Edward had him executed.

War was across the entire kingdom and alliances were made and broken. Treason was rife and no one could trust anybody. The Welsh had been voicing complaints regarding the Marcher Lords, especially against Mortimer, since 1316. The king had always been sympathetic to the Welsh, but he could do little to assist them because he was faced with a civil war, which was developing all around him. In February 1316 the Welsh took matters into their own hands and under Llywelyn Bren, the great-grandson of Ifor Bach, they rose in rebellion in Glamorgan. It was a short-lived affair and Llywelyn was captured and eventually executed at Cardiff in 1317.

Poor harvests compounded the problems and in 1316 the Scots had contacted Gruffudd Llywd of Tregarnedd, the chief recruiter of Welsh forces for the king between 1279 and 1314. It was their intention to form an alliance and fight the English in a common war. This came two years after the Scottish victory at Bannockburn, when morale was very high. However, Edward was alert to the fact that Scotland may invade Wales and the garrisons at many of the castles across the country were in a state of readiness.

There are some who believe that Gruffudd may have intimated his agreement to the Scottish suggestion, but lacking documentation as proof there is no way of ever knowing what his intentions really were. If Gruffudd was going to side with the Scots it would probably have been out of hostility towards the oppressive rule of Roger Mortimer of Chirk, justice of Carmathen and Caernarfon between 1316 and 1322, rather than treason against his king. Word somehow leaked out about the rumour of the Scottish-Welsh alliance and the implication of Gruffudd. He was arrested and imprisoned between 1316 and 1318, and could be considered extremely fortunate not to have been executed. Four years after his release, Gruffudd did rise in revolt in 1322, but not it must be stressed in full rebellion.

Although Gruffudd's rebellion was not a complete uprising, it did allow Edward the opportunity to move his forces to defeat the reform group which included the most powerful of all the Marcher Lords on the Welsh borders. Executions followed of the earl of Lancaster and Lord Denbigh, and the Mortimers were also imprisoned. The Despensers, father and son, were restored to position and it was they who held the real power in England. They also seized much land across Wales from Pembroke to Chepstow. The king was virtually emasculated and was ruler in name alone. Edward's wife, Queen Isabella, was absent in France on a mission for her husband. Whilst living there she became personally involved with Roger Mortimer of Wigmore, who had escaped to France in 1323. For three years they conspired to raise forces to invade England. On 24 September 1326, Isabella and Roger Mortimer invaded, forcing the king to retreat into Wales.

It was to prove to no avail and Edward was finally captured near Neath, probably at Pen-Rhys in the Rhondda, on 16 December 1326. He was taken to Berkeley castle where he was kept prisoner. The Despensers were executed and Isabella and Mortimer forced the king to abdicate, thereby allowing them to rule. The queen's son, Edward, was but a boy aged fourteen years, and too young to rule with any power. The fate of Edward II now rested on the whims of his unfaithful wife and her lover. News of a rescue attempt mounted by Rhys ap Gruffudd and other Welsh supporters, aimed at releasing the king was uncovered by Mortimer and the mission failed. The usurpers could not afford to leave the king alive and a plot was hatched to have him murdered at Berkeley castle. The exact method used to kill the king has never been satis-factorily answered; according to chroniclers no mark was found on the body

55   Carew castle was built in 1105 by Gerald of Windsor near the tidal estuary between
Pembroke and Kilgetty. It was originally a motte-and-bailey style but evolved into a walled castle
with towers. Its turbulent history involved service in many battles and wars

to indicate the cause of death. Edward was buried in St Peters monastery in
Gloucester. His tomb became a place of pilgrimage for the Welsh, and the
chronicler Walsingham wrote of: 'The remarkable way in which he [Edward
II] was revered by the Welsh'.

The new-found power of Isabella and Mortimer would only last for three
years after the murder of Edward II. In that time, Mortimer appointed himself
justice of Wales and seized the lordships between Pembroke and Denbigh. At
last, in 1320, at the age of seventeen years Edward was able to assert himself as
king and Mortimer was arrested in Nottingham. He was taken to Tyburn in
London, the traditional site of execution for traitors, where he was publicly
executed. Unable to punish his mother, she would live on as dowager until
1358. The Welsh had tried their best to help the late king and been severely
punished for their efforts by Mortimer who had had a number imprisoned for
their temerity.

So what of the castles in Wales at the time of all this turmoil and fighting?
With the establishment of the most powerful sites, it only remained for them
to be upgraded to incorporate the new developments in defensive designs
which were emerging. The castle at Cardigan, for example, had had its
gatehouse strengthened by the addition of twin towers between 1280 and

1300. Carew castle was also being extended around the 1300s and other castles, such as Carreg Cennan were being exchanged as favours for power support in the bloody wars during the reign of Edward II *(55)*. The walls of Llawhaden castle were being strengthened and further developed by Bishop David Martyn, but it was not attacked during the civil war in 1321 or later. In 1317 the castles of Dinefwr and Dryslwyn were given to Hugh Despenser by Edward II and during the civil war of 1321–1322 both were attacked. The keep and other parts of the castle at Dinefwr were badly damaged. When Edward III became king in 1330 he ordered a number of castles to be repaired, including Cilgerran, which in 1326 had been declared in ruins. Threat of a French invasion prompted a programme of repairing castles throughout Wales, and strengthening particularly those defences along the coast.

CHANGING DEFENCES AND SIEGE WARFARE EQUIPMENT

The defences at Kidwelly castle were also improved and greatly expanded as they began to incorporate defensive ideas gained from designs seen in the Middle East during the Crusades. Over the years it would come to represent a style in castle building referred to as 'walls within walls'. This was an extremely powerful style of castle building and would have far-reaching consequences. Welsh castles were sited near to natural obstacles such as rivers which were incorporated into their defences. When this was not possible, then a force of labourers would divert the course of a river to incorporate it into a castle's defences. This is exactly what had happened in 1277 when Rhuddlan castle was being built and a force of almost 1,000 men dug a canal to link the castle to the sea. Kidwelly was one of a number of castles to benefit from being sited by a river which protected its eastern flank, with a large ditch dug to protect its western flank. At Caerphilly castle the earl Gilbert of Gloucester set out to incorporate a series of man-made water obstacles around his castle in 1272. The level of the water could be adjusted by means of sluice gates and was a very advanced form of defensive measure. Water obstacles meant that the walls of a castle could not be tunnelled under to effect an entry, nor could scaling ladders be placed close to the walls for an assault. In turn, the garrison could stock the water with fish to supply food for the castle. At Beaumaris castle on Anglesey the drawbridge was built in such a way that a ship of 40 tonnes could dock by the gate to re-supply the castle whilst lying in the safety of the defences of the great fortification.

The site at Kidwelly was one of the most powerful castles in south Wales and dominated the River Gwendraeth, which had tidal access and could, therefore, like Beaumaris, be supplied by sea. In the early years of the four-teenth century Kidwelly's defences were improved on by Henry of Lancaster, who oversaw the building of a new gatehouse which was immensely strong and of an advanced design. Under his direction the stout gatehouse was built at the southern end of the ward to serve as an additional defence to the main entrance of the castle. It has been compared to those defences used at the large Edwardian castles in north Wales, such as Harlech and Beaumaris. The design of the new gatehouse was such than any attacker would have to negotiate the drawbridge, batter their way through two sets of doors and a portcullis. At this stage, whilst confined in the gateway, the attackers would have been vulnerable to the defenders, who could drop a range of material onto them by means of openings known as 'murder holes'. A similar series of protected openings from behind which the defenders could hurl projectiles at the attackers was a feature called machicolation. This was set high in the curtain walls and permitted the defenders to shoot arrows and drop objects onto the attackers at the base of the wall or tower under assault.

Contrary to popular belief boiling oil was never used against attackers because oil was a very precious commodity and hardly likely to be wasted by pouring on the heads of the enemy. A much simpler method was to drop sand that had been heated to intense temperatures. This would burn on touching the skin, also causing irritation as it worked under the armour and if it went into the eyes of the attackers they would be blinded. Another method of preventing attackers from coming too close was to drop quicklime powder which would both blind and burn, inducing a reluctance to assault the castle walls. Boiling water, spears and even simple heavy stones could all be used to break up an attack and deter any assault.

Castles in Wales, and indeed throughout Britain, were now being built in a form known as concentric style. Those castles built in north Wales by Edward I such as Beaumaris and Harlech were in this form and Pembroke castle, along with others, were being redeveloped to evolve into this shape also. In fact Pembroke castle also incorporated 'murder holes' in its defences within the gatehouse *(56)*. Towers were now being built in a round style in order to eliminate any 'blind spots' where an attacker could take shelter from the defenders' attentions and archers who would try to shoot them. Where square towers could not be converted to a round design the architects thickened the base by adding a feature termed as either a 'batter' or 'spur' which made the base of the tower less vulnerable to demolition and tunnelling. Curtain walls were now being raised to greater heights and used to enclose the grounds of a castle, and these were pierced by a series of towers to create the concentric pattern. The walls and towers could still be fitted with hourdings or bratticing, as used at Harlech castle, and which served as a platform from whence the defenders could observe the base of the tower they were in without exposing themselves to the enemy's archers. From such a vantage point they could drop missiles on to the attackers. The main drawback to such wooden structures is the fact that they were vulnerable to destruction by fire attack. When a castle was well supplied and its defences prepared for war, there was little the garrison

56 Pembroke castle with its defences, which had the base of the walls thickened to withstand artillery fire. These batters or spurs made the base of the towers and walls less vulnerable to the impact of stone projectiles

had to fear. The heavy catapults and trebuchets could batter the walls and archers could shoot against the defenders, but a well-motivated garrison could withstand most attacks. In such cases it would only be disease or starvation which would force a garrison to quit the castle.

Medieval siege warfare engines were called artillery and included devices such as the Perrier, ballista, trebuchet and the mangonel (57). Although called artillery they did not use gunpowder and relied instead on stored energy either through torsion or tension power as well as counterpoise. The ballista could be used both as an offensive and defensive weapon. In the defence it was mounted in a small tower and would have allowed the defenders of a castle to aim at individual targets such as mounted knights or the attackers' catapults if they were placed in the open and within range. The ballista was similar in design to a device used by the Romans, and the large arrow-like projectile would have been deadly at quite long ranges. The perrier was operated by men hauling on a series of ropes to launch a stone projectile. Whilst functional, its range was limited and the men operating such devices would have been vulnerable to the archers of the defenders and the ballista. The mangonel, also based on a Roman design called the '*onager*' or 'wild ass' because of the kick it gave on

57 Above   A recreated mangonel being prepared for use at Caerphilly castle. This shows how the compact, but very powerful, weapon could hurl stone projectiles over medium ranges to either demolish walls or throw quicklime over the defences to blind the garrison

58 Right   A recreated mangonel being prepared for use at Caerphilly castle

59 A recreated trebuchet showing how some of the designs could be of enormous size. This was a powerful device which could throw massive weights over considerable distances, including hurling diseased carcasses and quicklime to contaminate or injure the defenders

being operated, was a very different piece of equipment altogether *(58)*. It was a true catapult design and was used to throw stone projectiles to smash walls and crush any defender who happened to be in the impact area.

The trebuchet was the heavyweight in any attackers' arsenal and came in a range of sizes. It used a counterpoise system to operate its catapult action and by all accounts was impressive to see in use *(59)*. The loading method was very labour intensive and it hurled projectiles in a high arc to smash walls or throw them over the walls of a castle. A trebuchet fitted with, say, a throwing arm 50ft (15.2m) in length and a counterpoise weight of 20,000lbs (9,070kg) could be used to hurl a stone projectile weighing 300lbs (136kg) out to ranges of 300 yards (274m). Trebuchets could be used to throw clay pots filled with quicklime into the interior of a castle under attack in order to blind the garrison. Very large models of this powerful siege engine could be used to propel the carcasses of diseased animals into the grounds of a castle to spread sickness. These actions were both early forms of chemical and biological warfare and when used at the appropriate time could achieve very successful results and bring about the surrender of a garrison. Some castles were modified specifically to mount counter-siege engines such as catapults within their defences. For example at Beaumaris and Criccieth castles in north Wales, these sites had structures specially built for such a purpose. At Beaumaris the 'gunner's walk' some 12ft (3.7m) thick allowed a trebuchet to be mounted for use alongside archers. At Criccieth castle, the 'engine tower' was built for a similar purpose.

At this time a new, far more sinister weapon was beginning to emerge, which would ultimately prove more powerful than any catapult and bring about the end of castles as defensive centres. This range of weaponry was also referred to as artillery, but instead of ropes, it used the chemical power of gunpowder to propel very heavy projectiles, which could be stone or iron and caused much more damage on impact. This range of artillery, also termed cannons or bombards in the Middle Ages, was still in its nascent stage of development when Edward III ascended the throne, but he would come to use it in his army and later wars would see it become increasingly more powerful. Because catapults and gunpowder weapons were both termed as artillery there emerges a slight confusion over usage of the term *(60)*. For example, a minister's account from Pembroke castle *c*.1330, held in the Public Records Office refers to: '12 pairs of guns with one iron chain, 13s; one springald with wheels [stone-throwing machine], 6s 8d; 4 crossbows, 6d each; 4 old coats of mail, 3s 4d each.' The figures refer to the price of each item, but the actual reference to 'guns' is somewhat ambiguous. Whilst firearms were known to be in use at this time it is not clear whether these were guns in the real sense of the term. It seems unlikely that there would have been a requirement for such advanced weaponry in Wales at this time, and therefore one has to conclude that the term 'guns' is a misinterpretation of what was written at the time. The

60 Early gunpowder artillery was very unstable and expensive to deploy. In Wales such weaponry would be used against castles. In later campaigns weapons of enormous size were brought forward to pound at castle defences

reason for this assumption is that gunpowder artillery was extremely expensive and the men trained in its use would have been few in number. With Wales going through a very quiet period at this point in time there would have been no need, therefore, to deploy such expensive weaponry. This would not always remain the case and when artillery came to be used against castles later in the fourteenth century, the high walls would prove to be simply large, vulnerable targets.

EDWARD III

When Edward III asserted his power as king in 1330, he did not view Wales in the same liberal way as did his father and grandfather. In fact, if anything this Edward was suspicious of the Welsh and saw the land as a means of revenue to pay his creditors and to finance his wars. After all, the income from Wales, at the time when the lands were granted to Edward I in 1254 by Henry III, was estimated as being around £4,000 per year. In the intervening period of almost eighty years this had increased tremendously and would allow Edward III to sponsor his foreign wars. The country was rich in many commodities including food produced by farms, minerals such as lead, copper, iron and coal, horses and above all men who could serve as troops in the wars. Experienced troops would have to be recruited and these would prove a great asset to the new king's army. Welshmen had long been serving in the army of the king and they were regarded as among some of the finest troops, if somewhat unconventional and at times unpredictable. For example, in 1326 some 4,000 Welshmen were serving in Gascony and it would be from the survivors of such wars that the king could form a nucleus from around which a strong and reliable fighting force could be created. Welshmen had been used to recruit their fellow countrymen for service in the king's army for many years and they were greatly rewarded for this service.

Between 1279 and 1314 one of the main recruiting agents in Wales was Gruffudd Llwyd of Tregarnedd on Anglesey. Another Welshman who served in this role of recruiter was Rhys ap Gruffudd of Llansadwrn, who raised troops between 1310 and 1341. The ordinary Welshman had an understandable reluctance to serve under anyone other than a fellow Welshman and these figures would have been acceptable to them. In the years to come many thousands of Welshmen would go off to fight in the foreign wars which came to be known as the Hundred Years War. At this time the English did not entirely trust the Welsh and when localised fighting broke out in several parts

61 Re-enactors showing how troops of the period would have appeared. Armed with pole arms, swords and daggers, these are the infantrymen. They wear light armour which would have been acquired from victims at previous battles and includes helmets and padded jackets

62 Re-enactors showing how archers from the period were lightly equipped and concentrated on being flexible enough to move rapidly to any part of the battlefield. In some cases an archer could release over twelve arrows per minute, which meant even a moderate force could smother the defenders with a hail of arrows

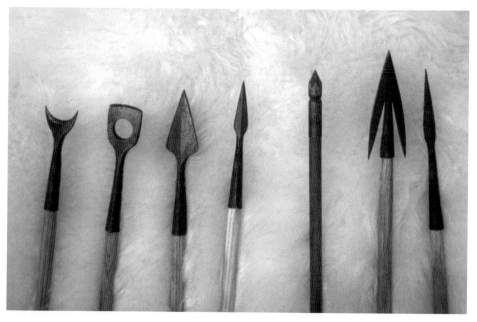

63 Several types of arrowhead, which could be fitted to the shaft of the arrow. This range includes broad head, 'bodkin' with its thin pencil-like appearance and 'swallow head', all of which could inflict terrible injuries

of the country they believed it to be a rebellion to oust them from Wales. One call which went out stated that: 'If the Welsh have their own way, there will shortly be not an Englishman alive in Wales.' The burgesses of Denbigh declared: 'The Welsh are now more prone than ever to rise against the king... the English of Denbigh dare not leave the town.' *(61)* This dread fear of Welsh intentions against the English spread and the burgesses of Caernarfon reported that: 'The Welsh are becoming arrogant and cruel and malicious towards the English.' In Rhuddlan the authorities believed that: 'the English will be exterminated from the land.' This series of events was unknown to those Welshmen serving in the king's army in France. Had they known about the situation it would probably have given them little cause for concern and there was, in any case, nothing they could do about the situation.

Even before Edward III became king, relations between France and England had been deteriorating over an extended period previous to hostilities breaking out into what is commonly referred to as the Hundred Years War. The war, which actually lasted 114 years, from 1337 to 1453, was the result of a typical feudal dispute, but almost from the very beginning was nationalistic in aspect. Despite its name the Hundred Years War did not consist of a single prolonged period of continuous fighting, but can instead be categorised into eight periods, with lengths of uneasy peace in between as a result of various treaties. The first episode is known as the Crecy Period, lasting between 1345 and 1347, during which time Edward raised an army of 30,000 men to invade France. His army comprised 4,000 men-at-arms, 10,000 archers, 6,000 Irish infantry and 10,000 Welsh infantry *(62)*. Before the invasion England and France had fought for several years a number of relatively small battles, originated by King Edward III raiding into France, establishing military bases and proclaiming himself king of France. At long last, the two protagonists came to face one another across a field just outside the small town of Crecy, which was to have serious and long-lasting implications in European history, not least because it was the first major land battle in a series of many engagements which would be fought between many generations of men.

On 26 August 1346 the army of Edward III consisted of about 3,000 men-at-arms and knights, 10,000 archers, and a number of others serving as infantrymen. Present on the battlefield were some 5,000 Welshmen, who were distinguished from the rest of his army by their uniform of green and white. This has been identified as being the first national uniform worn by any troops in European warfare. The French army numbered some 60,000 troops, of whom 12,000 were heavy cavalry, supported with a mercenary force of some 6,000 Genoese crossbowmen. The weather was inclement and there had been a brief but intense rain storm shortly before the opening of the battle, which was to have disastrous consequences for the French. The French with their numerical superiority were confident of an easy victory and proceeded to stage one cavalry charge after another. Despite their heavy armour protection, each successive assault was halted and broken by the withering hail of arrows put up by the force of archers in Edward's army. Armed with the longbow, even the most inexperienced archer was capable of shooting at least six arrows per minute, while the very experienced archers could shoot more than ten arrows per minute, to produce a veritable 'storm of arrows', which was more than sufficient to halt even the most determined cavalry charge *(63)*. The Genoese crossbowmen attempted to reply but the range was too long for their crossbow arrows to carry and the rain had slackened the strings of their weapons which further reduced the range of their arrows. The Welsh and English archers had kept their bowstrings dry during the rain storm and were able to shoot a deadly hail of arrows against the Genoese troops who broke rank and fled. This was the first in a series of battles where the Welsh longbow would have a telling effect on the enemy.

Over the coming years Welsh and English archers would dominate the battlefields in France and win great victories. At the battle of Poitiers, 19 September 1356, English and Welsh archers were deployed as part of a force of 6,000 men commanded by the king's son, Edward the Black Prince, and once more contributed to a great victory. Even with such great victories the Welsh were still regarded with some trepidation. Indeed, in his classic work, *A History of Wales*, the Welsh historian John Davies writes:

> The Welsh were troublesome soldiers; they tended to get drunk and to pillage and vandalize, and as they were accustomed to the savagery of racial conflict they were reluctant to conform to the conventions of dynastic warfare: they killed their prisoners instead of offering them for ransom.

Despite all this they were great fighters and because of their background were able to soldier on in the face of great adversity. Edward's reluctance to accept the Welsh as being equal among men did not prevent him from using the services of these self-same men as his troops.

The wars in France diverted attention away from Wales and the country seemed to relax in this atmosphere. The great Marcher Lords and other nobles from Wales were obliged to fight in these wars with their king. Sir Gregory Sais from Flintshire did service for his king, as did Sir Hywel ap Gruffydd who excelled in the use of the battleaxe to such a degree that he was termed Sir Hywel of the Axe. Whilst tales of great prowess of such men were being relayed back to Wales there was little, if any, evidence of profit returning to the country as a result of spoils of war. Some money was coming into the country from those in the service of the king, but more was going out of the country. Matters were made worse when the plague known as the Black Death came to Wales. The first victims of this disease in Wales were recorded in Carmarthen and Abergavenny during March 1349. There were to be two more visitations by the Black Death, which claimed one person in three as victims. Europe was devastated by the plague and Wales was affected as much as any other country at the time. This leads one to conclude that although in such a weakened state it may have been this disaster, combined with the fact that so many able-bodied men were serving abroad that prevented any uprising.

As the wars in France wore on so the king's attention continued to be diverted away from Wales. However, the fears of French invasion were rife and the castles across the country were kept in a high state of readiness. Garrisons were maintained and money was spent on the upkeep and improvement of castles in the event that the French should attack. Dinefwr had money allocated for the repair of the roof in 1353, but the work had still not been completed by 1360. There was also the fear that Welsh exiles would invade with the support of the French. One such threat was in the personage of Owain Lawgoch (Owain the Red Hand) who was the great-nephew of Llywelyn the Last and had strong claims to leadership of the Welsh. In 1369 Owain had a French fleet gathered at Harfleur but storms prevented it from sailing. In 1372 he received the not inconsiderable sum of 300,000 francs from the French to invade Wales, but in the event he got no further than the island of Guernsey in the Channel Islands, which he attacked on the grounds that it was a bailiwick of the English king. There was a popular following ready to meet him in Wales and he again posed a threat in 1378, which greatly alarmed the English. Owain was killed by an assassin, probably in a plot hatched by the English, and this very real threat to stability in Wales was removed at a stroke. The second half of the fourteenth century was a time of much confusion and the opportunity for people in power to exploit this to their own advantage was great. All the time the Hundred Years War, started in the reign of Edward III, was draining resources and as the fighting continued during the reign of Richard II it did not always necessarily go in favour of the king.

Edward III died in June 1377, having been pre-deceased by his wife, Queen Philippa in 1369. After her death Edward lost his sense of direction and reason for living. In fact, the shock of her death caused him to fall into bad health and his judgement in matters of national importance was severely impaired. The death of his warrior son, Edward the Black Prince, so named after the colour of his armour, in June 1376 merely added to the king's moroseness. It has been claimed by the historian Ralph A. Griffiths that Edward III was able to maintain calm in Wales even though disasters struck and the wars in France continued due to: 'the inspiration, example, and leadership of Edward III and the Black Prince, both of who embodied the chivalric virtues vaunted by the nobility and admired by society at large.' Edward III may have lacked personal trust in the Welsh, but he knew enough to present his son, Edward the Black Prince, to the country as the Prince of Wales in 1343, in the same gesture as Edward II was presented by his father in 1301. But with the death of the king and his natural heir, the title of king fell to Edward's grandson, the son of the

Black Prince, who would reign as Richard II. This was a great responsibility for a boy aged only ten years old. Almost from the beginning his reign was to be marred, mainly by quarrelling family members.

RICHARD II

By this stage the wars in France were still absorbing great amounts of money, men and material. The battle of Poitiers had been won in 1356 but the French had introduced new tactics, which included a refusal to give battle unless it was advantageous to them, and little had been achieved by England since then. With no news of fresh victories and a peasants' revolt in London, the boy king was faced with many troubles. One factor going in the king's favour was the fact that Wales was still peaceful. Despite the fact that a French invasion of Wales was feared, the wars in Europe had dragged on for so long without any attack, it was inevitable that defences would be allowed to slip. In 1386 the defences at Tenby, right on the coast, were reported to be in a bad state of repair. The gates were decayed, the curtain walls were fallen and other buildings were collapsed. However, not all was bad news, because at Haverfordwest castle we learn that from around the same time things were very different. In 1387 new stables were erected at the site and an inventory of the arms and armour tells us the castle was equipped with: '2 cannon and 6 handguns plus a stock of stone balls for them to fire and a barrel of gunpowder'. It is safe to believe that gunpowder weapons would have been used to some degree in Wales in the first-half of the fourteenth century but it is not until the report from Haverfordwest castle that we are given the earliest reliable account of such weapons being stored in any quantity in Wales.

It is not surprising, because by now gunpowder weapons had been in use since around 1326, and at Crécy in 1346 Edward III is believed to have used some cannon. Soldiers returning to Wales after serving in the Hundred Years War would have had experience of such weapons and their knowledge would be crucial to the future of the castle. The coming of gunpowder weapons and the men to operate such powerful weapons would ultimately signal the end of the great medieval castle as a symbol of power. In an effort to reduce vulnerability to cannon fire, castle walls were made even thicker at the base, and permanent outworks were being constructed at a distance from the main walls. One type of feature to be developed for this purpose was known as the 'barbican', which was really a fortified extension of the gateway, and appeared at sites such as Carreg Cennen castle, Pembroke and others. In such positions cannon and lighter firearms could be emplaced, and used by defenders to protect themselves during a siege. These modifications were slow to arrive in Wales and even then were not always incorporated into castles across the country. The reason for this was simple, because with only internal national boundaries to mark the borders of Scotland and Wales, it was perceived that there was no need to strengthen every castle. However, internal fighting such as the Wars of the Roses and localised threats would lead to a gradual redesigning of a range of castles. Indeed, by the end of the century, artillery had all but rendered obsolete those traditionally built medieval fortifications. The tall, straight walls were a target just waiting to be attacked by gunners and walls of those unmodified sites meant there was nowhere in which large cannon suitable for counter-battery operations could be sited. From the defenders' point of view the walls of the castles had to be modified and examples of this are evident at Carreg Cennan, Pembroke and Raglan castles. Here the openings were 'splayed' to allow gunpowder weapons to be moved and aimed at targets, while at the same time still giving protective cover to the defenders *(64)*.

Pembroke castle had its defences improved to withstand the effects of artillery in the fourteenth century by the simple expedient of building up banks of earth in front of the stone walls to absorb the impact of the projectiles. At Laugharne castle the defences were updated and improved, as was the gatehouse, and some of the walls were increased in height. At Carreg Cennen we learn from accounts written by Roger Aylward *c.*1369–1370 of improvements made to the castle there:

> The replacement of the middle drawbridge… The cutting and trimming of joists and shingles in the king's forest of Pedoul, for the roofing of the hall and other houses within the castle… An iron bar for the outer gate… The walling up of two watch towers near the middle gate, and of one watch tower beyond the king's chamber… The walling up of an opening in the prison below the middle gate… Provision of locks for the wicket of the outer gate, for the inner gate, and for the doors of the hall…

Other work was also completed which came to the grand amount of £4 1s 3d (more than £2,000 in modern terms). This document, which is kept in Public Record Office, tells us wages were being paid to three men maintaining watch in the castle 'on account of the enemies from France' who might land with Owain Lawgoch.

Wales at this time was under pressure to supply finances in the form of taxes to support the wars in France, which showed no sign of coming to an end. Fortunately for Richard, the peasants' revolt in England, which had been as a result of such taxes did not spread to Wales. On that issue at least the king could count himself extremely fortunate, because the rebellion had numbered some 100,000 strong led by Wat Tyler and Jack Straw. In 1377 Richard was guided by his uncle, John of Gaunt, duke of Lancaster, and this arrangement would last until 1385, the year in which Richard would lead a fruitless and wasteful campaign into Scotland.

In 1389 Richard finally asserted himself as king in his own right, declaring: 'I am of full age to govern my house, and my household and also my realm...'. Richard had to move cautiously for he had many enemies and opposition towards him was strong and included some of the most powerful magnates in the land. Until this time Richard had not had any great dealings with Wales or the Welsh people. However in that year he sought to ingratiate himself with them and build up a loyal following in north Wales. Among those from whom he won support was the family of Tudur ap Goronwy of Anglesey. Richard was an imaginative, shrewd and masterful ruler, as proven in his ability to talk down the massive rebellion facing him in London during 1381. For the most part he was preoccupied with his own troubles, which included threats to his monarchy and left little time to worry about interfering with Wales. When civil war broke out Richard was vulnerable and weakened. He had shown himself to be capable of making wise moves in campaigns, for example when he led a force into Ireland in 1394–1395, which was largely successful. In 1396 he managed to broker a truce with truce with France to halt the wars and even went as far as marrying the eight-year-old Isabelle of Valois to reaffirm this move. But in domestic affairs he overreached himself when he turned on his nobles and exiled the earls of Warwick, Derby and Nottingham and had the earl of Gloucester murdered. When John of Gaunt, duke of Lancaster died in 1399 Richard turned on his late uncle's son, Henry Bolingbroke, sending him into exile and seized the possessions of the family of Lancaster, thereby making another powerful enemy.

Henry Bolingbroke believed he had a claim to the throne as the grandson of Edward III, through the late king's third son, John of Gaunt. In 1399, when Richard was campaigning once more in Ireland, Henry Bolingbroke made his move to seize the throne from his cousin and in July he landed at Ravenspur on the coast of Yorkshire. He was assured of support from the powerful Percy family, whom Richard had also aggrieved, and further support to his claim was also growing. Learning of this, Richard returned, and on 28 July 1399 landed on the coast near Haverfordwest where the castle dominated the whole town. However, he did not have a strong following for his cause and he was forced to move across Wales from one castle to another. One of these was Conwy castle where Richard had moved with as few as 100 followers. This was one of the castles built by Edward I and designed to be capable of being defended by a relatively small garrison. In theory, therefore, Richard's followers should have been sufficient in number to hold the castle. However, in their weakened state and with no preparations having been made to place the castle in order to withstand a siege they were left with no choice other than to receive a deputation from Henry Bolingbroke.

The gates were opened to permit entry by the earl of Northumberland, Henry Percy, as the representative of Henry Bolingbroke. The terms discussed included the matter that the Richard would be allowed to return to office if he agreed to rule in a manner more befitting a king. It was an attempt to move Richard away from Conwy castle where he would have had better communication with any support coming from Ireland. Richard moved towards Flint castle where he met with Henry who, being in the stronger position to dictate terms, treated his cousin with great respect. However, he was determined that Richard should not continue as regent of England and Wales. The king was made prisoner on 19 August by his cousin's supporters. Richard was declared to be dethroned in September and taken to the Tower of London before being removed to Pontefract castle in West Yorkshire, where he is believed to have been murdered by means of suffocation either in late December 1399 or early January 1400. The castles built in the north of Wales over 100 years earlier to protect the king's realm in Wales had proven their worth in times gone by, but in the case of Richard they were to prove his undoing. Despite having been abandoned by most of his supporters he did have a small following still after his seizure. Their action proved too little too late and they were defeated in battle at Cirencester in December 1399.

Henry had wasted no time and as soon as Richard had been stripped of his rule declared himself king on 29 September. He had taken the throne of England and would rule as Henry IV. He presented his son Henry, who had been born in Monmouth in 1387, to the Welsh people and on 15 October 1399, invested him with the principality of Wales. He believed he had made a wise move but he had angered powerful lords in Wales and they were far from pleased with the situation *(65)*. In truth, the new king's troubles with Wales were only just beginning. The squabbles between the cousins over the kingship of the country was of no importance to the Welsh, who had to accept as king whoever emerged victorious from this in-fighting which was so familiar to them. But that did not mean they had to accept the new king meekly and without any demonstration of their disaffection.

Among Richard's followers taken at Flint castle was a Welshman of noble descent by the name of Owain Glyn Dwr (sometime written as either Owen Glendwr or Owen Glendower and other variants of the spelling). He had been loyal to the king, having been knighted in 1387, and served on the campaigns to Scotland. Despite a deposition by the dethroned king, Owain's estates were seized by Lord Grey de Ruthyn. Owain, who had hoped to be allowed to live on his family estates, complained to parliament with the support of the bishop of St Asaph. He did not receive any redress to his complaint about the actions of Lord Grey. Even so, he still believed he could be allowed to settle in peace, but it was not to be so. Lord Grey had kept back a writ, which summoned Owain Glyn Dwr and other barons to the banner of Henry IV for a campaign against the Scots. The king departed for his expedition against Scotland but Glyn Dwr did not join the force and Lord Grey seized more lands, which provoked outrage and Glyn Dwr vowed to expel the invaders from his lands. Taking up arms in the summer of 1400 he moved to take English prisoners and

64 Left A 'splayed' window, seen here at Beaumaris castle. This modified opening in the curtain wall was designed for use of gunpowder weapons, including firearms and artillery. The wide internal angle allowed the defender to follow the target, yet the external opening was still very narrow

65 Right King Henry IV, who presented his son Henry to the Welsh as the 'Prince of Wales' in October 1399 and was the cause of so much resentment. He would campaign into Wales and fight against a powerful and wily adversary in the person of Owain Glyn Dwr

even marched into those lands held by Lord Grey. After a period of relative calm during the reign of Richard II, Wales was once more on the brink of rebellion.

By 1400 the fighting in France had been almost continuous for over sixty years. There had been campaigns into Scotland and many Welshmen had accompanied the English army in these wars. With such an intense period of military activity it was inevitable that many Welshmen who had survived these battles had built up much tactical experience. These men had served as the formidable archers who had beaten the French at Crecy and Poitiers, and even as infantrymen in the massed ranks to receive cavalry charges from heavily armoured knights. As word of Glyn Dwr's growing rebellion began to spread across the country so many of these villeins (feudal serfs) travelled from England to return to Wales to lend their support. Having experience of large-scale medieval warfare, such men no longer used their age-old tactics of unconventional ambush and night attack. But that is not to say they had forgotten how to use such tactics; they would still not fail to use them if the opportunity arose. Armour and weaponry had also advanced and many of these men returning to Wales at this time were equipped with these better and stronger weapons. Compared to earlier rebellions against the English, these Welshmen were better prepared and armed. Over the next fifteen years or so, the English would come to fear the Welsh as never before.

Glyn Dwr would instil a new vigour into his countrymen and the English would accredit him with having mystical powers. Some came to believe that he was the personification of the legend predicted by the mythical Merlin from the stories of King Arthur and that here was: 'the moldwarp accursed of God's own wrath'. In Owain Glyn Dwr, here was the Welsh dragon who would destroy King Henry and end the English control of Wales. In this last year of the fourteenth century the English would, according to the historian and chronicler Holinshed, come to endow Glyn Dwr with supernatural, almost mystical powers: 'Through art-magic, he caused such foul weather of winds, tempest, rain, snow and hail to be raised for the annoyance of the king's army, that the like had not been heard of.' At a time when men were greatly superstitious such rumours would abound and from them would grow a strong reluctance, bordering on fear, among the English who did not wish to fight in Wales. As one contemporary from the period would come to write:

> *Beware of Wales, Jesus Christ must us keep,*
> *That it make not our child's child weep,*
> *Nor us also, if so it go this way*
> *By unwariness; since that many a day*
> *Men have been afraid of there rebellion…*

Wales was not only the centre for rebellion, it was also the route through which a French invasion might attack England. One is inclined to remember the words written in a letter by Master James of St Georges, the builder of the great castles in north Wales, which was addressed to Edward I around 1294 or 1295: 'You know well that Welshmen will be Welshmen even if they appear to be pacified'. Had Henry IV known about the comments in this letter he would have been well advised to heed their almost prophetic words from over 100 years earlier.

5

THE FIFTEENTH
CENTURY

On 16 September 1400 Owain ap Gruffydd Fychan, or as he is known to history Owain Glyn Dwr, was proclaimed Prince of Wales at Glyndyfrdwy in Merioneth. With this self-proclaimed declaration the path towards a Welsh revolt against English rule was laid, and it proved to be a war which would have a profound and long-lasting effect on the country. Owain Glyn Dwr was, at the time of this proclamation an important landowner with property at Glyndyfrdwy and Sycharth in Clwyd, which provided him with an annual income of £200. He was descended from Welsh ruling dynasties and an experienced soldier, known to have served with King Richard II during his Scottish campaigns in 1385 and 1387. It was not by accident that he was thrust into leadership for what would become the last great rebellion in Wales.

Glyn Dwr's ancestors are recorded in the chronicles at various times, and are mentioned as having been related to the earl of Arundel, lord of Chirk and Oswestry. His father was Gruffudd Fychan ap Madog, baron of Glyndyfrdwy and Cynllaith Owain in north-east Wales and descended from the kings of Powys. He is also understood to have been at one time a steward of the lordship of Oswestry. His mother, Helen, was the daughter of Thomas Llywelyn ab Owain, whose family was descended down the royal line of Deheubarth. Even his grandmother was descended from the Lestrange family, a leading household of the Marchers.

The exact date of Glyn Dwr's birth has never been conclusively substantiated. Some records state 1350 to be the year, whilst others place it at the slightly later date of 1354. It is purely an academic point and the question of only a few years one way or the other in the recording of his birth is but a minor triviality in the overall scheme of things. What we do see from his parentage is the fact that Glyn Dwr was very obviously of royal lineage. In society of the time, this placed him within a privileged class structure and he would have been known as an 'uchelwr' or 'high man'. Here was the man whose actions and deeds would come to cause so many problems to the English as he united Wales in what was to be the last great revolt. His property at Sycharth was a motte-and-bailey defensible site, which, by all accounts, was not built to a particularly strong design. According to the description left us by the court poet of the day, Iolo Goch, Sycharth was more concerned with producing food for consumption at court and states there was: 'No want, no hunger, no shame; Nor thirst are ever at Sycharth.'

His early life is rather fragmented, but his formative life and his rise in position are recorded in much better detail. He is understood to have spent time in London, where he is said to have studied law at the Inns of Court. Some accounts of his life disagree with this fact, but in the main most records seem to perpetuate this story, which leads one to conclude that there must be some element of truth in the tale. In 1384, Glyn Dwr is recorded as serving in the garrison of Berwick-upon-Tweed in Northumberland, under the command of Sir Gregory Sais, a fellow Welshman. In the following year, 1385, Glyn Dwr is recorded as fighting for Richard II in his Scottish campaign. Later he is known to have served in a number of military campaigns, including a naval action against the French in 1387, which would place his age as being around mid-thirties during the reign of Richard II. All of this experience in warfare would later be put to good use. The fact that Glyn Dwr had survived so much was a testimony to his fighting skills and his military prowess.

At the time of Owain Glyn Dwr's proclamation as Prince of Wales in 1400, the Hundred Years War was still being fought between England and France. England was itself only just recovering from civil war, which had seen the throne being seized from Richard II by his cousin Henry Bolingbroke who would rule as Henry IV. In fact it was probably Henry's attention being occupied by the fighting in France which allowed the Welsh to make their timely move to rise in rebellion. The English army was also weakened in numbers for home service because many of its resources had been drawn away to supply those troops in France. Indeed with so many distractions, along with other affairs of state, including the threat of further civil war, it was no wonder that the forces were able to gather in Wales.

Richard II was declared to be dead and although a body was shown in public there was allegedly no mark of violence on it and many believed he had been murdered on the orders of his cousin. If this was the case it certainly would not be the first time that regicide had been committed in England. The chronicler Froissart wrote: 'How Richard died and by what means I could not tell when I wrote this chronicle.' This led to rumours abounding about the king's true fate and stories began to circulate that he had escaped being murdered by Sir Piers Exton and that he had fled to Scotland where he was being held by the Regent Albany. All this was purely circumstantial, but it still did not prevent an uprising against Henry IV in an effort to get Richard restored.

Among those who chose to disbelieve the fact that Richard was no longer alive were the earls of Salisbury, Huntingdon, Kent and Despenser. They moved to kidnap Henry whilst he was in residence at Windsor castle over Christmas 1399, but they failed when their intended target fled after being warned of the attempt on his life. Rumours of Richard's survival would continue to circulate for at least another four years before the matter was finally put to rest. In fact one of those who also believed in the miraculous survival of Richard was Owain Glyn Dwr himself.

In 1400 Henry was fully in control and composed enough to begin a campaign to quell unrest which was growing in the north of England and even move into Scotland. In September the Welsh took Henry by surprise when they began their opening moves towards a full rebellion against the English. Incensed with hatred against the English for all the excesses of opposition, the Welsh sided with Glyn Dwr as their great leader. Although he had been taken unawares, Henry quickly recovered his composure and led a force into Wales. He was an energetic man with a forceful nature able to command troops on campaign.

It was not by mere chance that Glyn Dwr became the latest war leader to command his people in battle against the English. As early as the 1380s there were men of high position who were preparing him for a time when he would lead his country into war. Poets, such as Iolo Goch, sang: '*Barwn, mi a wn dy ach*' (Baron I know your lineage), for in their opinion Glyn Dwr was the '*yr edling o hen genhedlaeth*'. Translated this meant he was 'the aetheling of an ancient lineage'. The Welsh were convinced they had in him a great leader, and in return he did not disappoint them. In his favour were his experiences of warfare gained whilst in the service of Richard II and these would come to stand him in good stead. In the words of the Chinese military theorist, Sun Tzu, from the fifth century BC, 'Know the enemy and know yourself; in a hundred battles you will not be in danger.' Another of Sun Tzu's dictums was to avoid battle and: 'To defeat the enemy without fighting is the peak of excellence.' It is unlikely that Glyn Dwr knew of these maxims but in his war against the English he would apply both these ideals. After all, it was the Welsh way to withdraw to the hills when they were at a disadvantage and Glyn Dwr certainly knew his enemy because he had served in their army.

In an aggrieved state, Owain Glyn Dwr sought the support of Henry IV in his claims to have his lands restored, which had been seized by Lord Reginald de Grey of Ruthin. But when the king rejoined against Glyn Dwr he felt further wronged and betrayed, thus his anger grew more fierce. The reason for Glyn Dwr's revolt has traditionally been explained as stemming from this territorial dispute between himself and Reginald de Grey, combined with his refusal to serve the king in Scotland. Disputes of this nature between neighbouring lords were nothing new and in itself would have been unlikely to have sparked off a war. However, with much dissension concerning the way in which Henry had seized the monarchy in England and the Hundred Years War still being fought in France, Glyn Dwr must have sensed the time was right to strike back and claim Welsh political independence from England. It has been opined that the revolt may have been planned for as early as 1399, to support Richard II, who was popular in Wales, in his fight against Henry Bolingbroke.

The real reason may be seen somewhere between all of the events unfolding at the time, with Glyn Dwr's lack of personal support from the king being the final insult. This may be partly the reason, but one has to remember that the Welsh had long been dissatisfied with English clerics in Welsh churches and the continued increase in taxes to support the war in France. One churchman to speak in favour of Owain Glyn Dwr at the time of these grievances was the bishop of St Asaph, who demanded that the Welshman's lands be given back. The words, apparently spoken by Lord Grey added further insult to injury when he stated: 'What care we for these barefoot rascals.' He would later come to care greatly about these 'barefoot rascals'. It was sensed that the time was now right for the Welsh to take action and Glyn Dwr was considered to be the man for the role, a feeling strengthened by his military experience and his family lineage. Even Lewis Byford, later to be elected bishop of Bangor in 1404, openly supported Glyn Dwr in his actions.

On 16 September 1400 the banner of Welsh revolt was raised at Glyndyfrdwy, and on the same day Glyn Dwr established a parliament at Machynlleth *(66)*. Over the coming week Glyn Dwr's forces attacked eight towns in the north-east of Wales, and he directed a force of only 250 men against Ruthin castle near Denbigh, which was held by Reginald de Grey, who had so angered him. It was not just a personal act of aggression, for by attacking such a strong castle the Welsh were showing that they were a force to be reckoned with. Ruthin castle was one of the fortifications built during the reign of Edward I, and had already been involved in earlier Welsh wars. Over the years it had been considerably strengthened and expanded. The castle had originally been a stronghold for the Welsh, but now under the lordship of the de Greys it had been developed into a formidable defensive structure, the walls of which were overlooked by several round towers. One side of the castle angled outwards from where the central and eastern towers allowed the defenders an excellent view of the main gateway.

During the fighting, the town of Ruthin was set on fire and all but three buildings were destroyed, but the garrison of the castle maintained their discipline and remained at their posts. The castle was invested and the Welsh troops of Glyn Dwr set about the task of laying siege to the castle. However, he was wise enough to know that when such a siege situation developed, it deprived the rest of the army of troops, who could otherwise be used in other actions against an enemy. Ruthin castle was not captured on this occasion but over the next two years it would become the centre of attention for Glyn Dwr, which indicates the level of importance and bitter hatred that he attached to the site.

66 The building in Machynlleth where Owain Glyn Dwr established one of his parliaments. Here many subjects were debated and war plans were also laid

The fact that he was able to maintain military action against such a formidable castle indicates that Glyn Dwr was confident in the manpower available to him in order to permit the detaching of numbers of men away from his army to continue the sporadic investment of Ruthin castle.

In the meantime, Henry IV had not been slow to react to Glyn Dwr's aggressive actions and had mobilised an army to march into north Wales in October 1400. This force encountered some rebels who, realising they were in no position to fight, decided to surrender, whilst others paid homage and were pardoned. In September a column of English troops marching out of Shropshire surprised and attacked a force of Welsh, which they defeated. Glyn Dwr was quick to recognise the fact that he was not yet strong enough to face the king's army in open battle and chose instead to avoid direct conflict. Among his allies were his cousins, Gwilym and Rhys ap Tudur ap Goronwy, who headed an uprising into Anglesey.

Like his predecessors, Glyn Dwr would prove to be a master at using ambushes and launching surprise attacks. He could also draw on his military experience and knowledge of the Welsh hills, from where he could conduct a successful partisan war, designed to wear down the English will to fight.

67 Conwy castle on the River Conwy, overlooking the northern end of the Mennai Straits, and one of the castles built during the reign of Edward I. Capable of withstanding a siege, the forces of Owain Glyn Dwr would seize it by subterfuge in Easter 1401

However, it would not always prove possible for the Welsh to employ their preferred tactic of avoiding battle in open ground. During the rebellion they would come to engage the army of the king on the battlefield, sometimes gaining victory and other times learning from their defeat. With his remaining lands confiscated by the king, Glyn Dwr lacked a safe haven into which he could retreat and this led him to withdraw deep into the mountains. His troops had not been defeated in battle, they were not beaten and none had been captured. However, some Welsh did elect to make peace with the king. Henry's son, Henry of Monmouth, was the latest English Prince of Wales and he established his base of operations at Chester. Henry Percy (Hotspur) the earl of Northumberland who had supported Henry IV in his war against Richard had been rewarded for his services by being granted high offices in the principality. To most people the insurrection was assumed to be at an end.

However, it was far from over and although Glyn Dwr, by now declared an outlaw and rebel by the king, had withdrawn to the hills he was already planning his next moves. The hills in central Wales are remote and inaccessible and from these fastnesses he was able to plot his coming campaign. The first attacks of late 1400 had only been the opening moves in a war which was to

68 The powerful defences of Conwy castle. Despite this imposing view, Glyn Dwr's forces entered the castle dressed as carpenters and captured it without a fight

become ever more fierce. Glyn Dwr made his next move during Easter 1401 when he once more attacked sites with the aid of his allies Rhys and Gwilwym Tudur ap Goronwy, and together moved on to Conwy castle *(67)*. On Good Friday, 1 April, they took the powerful castle despite its great defences with ease, by simply posing as carpenters and entering it when the garrison was at church. This action of subterfuge was an audacious deception and has come to be looked on by some historians as being a token gesture, which it may have been, but it did prove to the king that the Welsh should never be underestimated. However, one cannot help but admire the cunning simplicity of the plan that lost the king a powerful castle in north Wales *(68)*. The chronicler Adam of Usk wrote of the event:

> Gwilym ap Tudor and Rhys ap Tudor, brothers, natives of the Isle of Anglesey or Mona, because they were unable to obtain the king's pardon for the rebellion of the aforesaid Owain, on Good Friday of the same year seized the castle of Conwy, well stocked as it was with arms and provisions. Having slain the two warders through the subtlety of a certain carpenter who pretended to come to his work as usual, and entering with forty other men, they held it as a stronghold.

The Welsh prince was tireless in his leadership and an inspiration to his followers. The fighting which developed in 1401 continued sporadically throughout the year, Glyn Dwr all the time still refusing to give outright battle. In June that year an exception was made when a Welsh force of some 400 men were surprised at night by a superior force of 1,500 troops at Mynydd Hyddgen on the slopes of Pumlumon in northern Cardiganshire. Accounts vary as to the origin of the attacking force. Most references say it was English while a few accounts claim it was made up from Flemish troops, possibly from the *Landsker* settlers. There is, of course, another possibility that the attacking force comprised both English and Flemish troops. The outnumbered Welsh force fought valiantly and drove off the attackers. It was an example of how fiercely the Welsh could fight when called on to do so and not simply withdraw into the hills. At this point Glyn Dwr knew his limitations and maintained his avoidance tactics, which so frustrated the English king that he ordered the sacking of the abbey at Strata Florida. Indeed, the two sides would only meet in open battle very few times during the time of the whole rebellion, with varying results.

In October 1401 Henry was in Wales for the second time that year, but he was still unable to suppress the rebellion. Each time his troops approached, the Welsh merely adopted their age-old tactics and simply fell back into the hills where the English were either unable or unwilling to venture. In November Glyn Dwr's forces were at Caernarfon and his fortunes appeared to have changed dramatically from only the year before when he was almost starving as he hid out in the bleak hills. Now his followers were flocking to his banner and he was receiving widespread support either from troops or supplies to feed his forces. The king's army was not able to sustain itself in the field and suffering from lack of food, exhausted and weather-beaten the English were forced to fall back from Wales. The chronicler, Adam of Usk, wrote of the events:

> That October with the whole of North Wales, Ceredigion and Powys siding with him, Owain Glyndwr fiercely attacked with fire and sword the English living in those parts together with their towns... Because of this the English invaded those parts with a powerful force, plundering and destroying with fire, famine and sword, leaving them a wilderness without sparing neither child nor church nor the monastery of Strata Florida, where the king himself lodged, and kept their horses in the church, chancel, even up to the altar, and destroyed even the communion plate, and carried to England over a thousand children of both sexes to be their servants.

The civilian population would suffer the most in this war as each side campaigned across Wales.

On 2 November 1401, the Welsh forces moved on to invest Caernarfon, but they failed to make any impression, and Owain Glyn Dwr marched against

69   Caernarfon castle was attacked by the forces of Owain Glyn Dwr in November 1401. The siege lasted into 1402 and the great castle was only captured when the Welsh bribed the garrison to open the gates. Glyn Dwr used it as a base of operations against the English until 1406

the great castle at Harlech and laid siege to its imposing structure *(69)*. Adam of Usk wrote of Glyn Dwr's failed attack against Caernarfon:

> The day following All Saints Day as Owain intended to attack Caernarfon, there in the presence of a huge crowd, he raised his banner, a red dragon on a white background; but because those inside attacked him he was put to flight, losing three hundred of his men.

The garrison at Harlech comprised twenty men-at-arms and eighty archers, and with plenty of supplies coming through, along with reinforcements, they would manage to hold out for over three long years. During the siege the castle received a supply of gunpowder weapons including artillery in 1402. These managed to keep the Welsh besiegers at bay, and they were forced to try and wear down the garrison through starvation, which also increased the risk of disease, the most dreaded aspect of any siege. Even after all their privations the garrison was determined to hold on to their possession, despite some of their number deserting, and the castle was an English outpost in countryside dominated by the Welsh rebels. No doubt frustrated by their inability to seize the castle, the Welsh finally resorted to the unusual expedient of simply bribing the garrison to quit their posts and open the castle to them. Glyn Dwr took up residency in the castle, which he used as a base of operations for the next four years as he campaigned against the English.

Four years later, following a siege between 1408 and 1409 Harlech castle would be retaken by an English force of over 1,000 men, commanded by Sir Gilbert Talbot, who had gunpowder artillery. One of these weapons, named 'The King's Daughter', could fire cannonballs of 22" in diameter, which would have made short work of parts of the castle's defences. It was this display of force by superior weaponry, along with a similar action earlier at Aberystwyth castle in 1407, which would finally break the back of the Welsh rebellion in 1409.

In 1402 Glyn Dwr's war chest was swollen when he received a not insubstantial sum of money for the ransom of Reginald de Grey. This was a much-needed source of income, because his army had to be paid if they were to remain loyal and equipment had to be purchased. The capture of such an important personage as Reginald de Grey had only been possible when he left his castle in an attempt to engage the Welsh in open warfare. Eventually, in 1402 his forces met those of Glyn Dwr's in battle at Vyrnwy. For the Welsh it was a great victory, capturing as they did Reginald de Grey, whose importance they realised, and they imprisoned him in Snowdonia where he was held to ransom for the sum of £650,000. In a separate action fought on 22 June 1402 at Pilleth or Bryn Glas (meaning Blue Hill) on the River Lugg, to the north of Radnor, the Welsh also launched one of their traditional surprise attacks on an English force as it was making its way through a mountain defile. The battle was another outstanding Welsh victory and saw over 1,100 English troops killed. The Welsh had a number of women following their forces and they fell upon the slain English and mutilated their bodies. This caused an outcry because it infringed the codes of warfare, but there was nothing to be done. No doubt the women were venting their wrath in the only way possible to them, which was to attack the dead enemy. Again the chronicles of Adam of Usk support the account:

On St Alban's Day near Knighton in Wales, a hard battle was fought between the English under Sir Edumnd Mortimer and the Welsh under Owain Glyndwr and almost eight thousand were killed, and Owain was victorious. And, oh, after the fortunes of war my lord Sir Edmund by name was taken prisoner. And because his property was stolen from him by his enemies in England, and so he was kept from paying for his release so that he could escape more easily from the pains of his imprisonment; we know from what is said, that he married the daughter of the same Owain and had a son, Lionel, and three daughters.

Owain Glyn Dwr was personally leading the forces at Pilleth near Knighton when they captured Sir Edmund Mortimer, commanding the English force, who it was thought would make for a good ransom. But being of bloodline to the deposed Richard II, it was realised that he was of no relevance to Henry IV and therefore had no ransom value. The ransom for de Grey had been paid, which led to the ruination of the family and provided money for Glyn Dwr to continue his war against the English. But there was no money forthcoming for Mortimer. Edmund Mortimer, we know from other sources, befriended Owain Glyn Dwr, promising that he would support and ensure the prince's rights in Wales. To seal this promise he married Glyn Dwr's daughter, Catrin. It has been supposed that the Welsh may even have possessed a limited number of weapons to form units equipped with gunpowder artillery, which had been supplied by the French. If this was so, then it would certainly have given the Welsh the means to reply to English artillery and assist in sieges at the sites of various castles, such as Cardiff and Aberystwyth, both of which were extremely powerful.

The exact size and strength of Glyn Dwr's army cannot be established with any great certainty because it would have fluctuated according to the action and season during which a particular campaign was being conducted. It is believed that from time to time he was able to assemble forces of up to 8,000 men, almost certainly with the aid of French mercenaries. To counter this the English dispatched armies of 4,000 men, which was a force of considerable size for service at home and certainly believed to be powerful enough to deal with the rebels. When one considers that armies of 5,000–6,000 men were being sent to fight in the Hundred Years War at this time, this number gives some indication of the level of importance attached to trying to suppress the Welsh. The onus of supplying these troops invariably fell on those counties bordering Wales, in particular the west Midlands. However, the troops were never happy about serving in Wales and in September 1403 Henry was informed by a minister that: 'You will not find a single gentleman who will stop in your said country.' At this time the population has been estimated to have been approximately 250,000 spread out over the remote countryside. Wales had been decimated by the Black Death and the populace had not yet recovered. Glyn Dwr was able to call on the resources of local rulers, not all of whom would have been willing to support his cause, but most would have done so mainly because it was a common enemy, the English, they were fighting. Furthermore, the Welsh were fighting in their own country and often in the regions of their own family settlements. In addition, Glyn Dwr was able to attract mercenaries and even enter an alliance with France, England's enemy during the seemingly endless Hundred Years War.

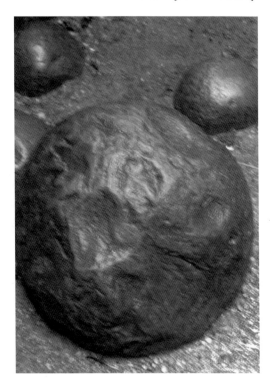

70 Projectiles fired by early gunpowder artillery were carved from stone. These were fired at Harlech castle during the great siege of 1408 when the English besieged the castle and captured it, along with the inhabitants which included Glyn Dwr's wife and family

ARTILLERY IN THE WARS

Gunpowder artillery had certainly been in use for more than seventy years by the time of Glyn Dwr's uprising and with his military experience, even regardless of, he could not have failed to be aware of its capability. It was being used by both sides during the Hundred Years War in France and some mercenaries may well have been paid to come to Wales with their weapons through funds provided by ransom money. Indeed, it is quite possible that when Glyn Dwr entered negotiations to secure assistance from France they may well have sent some artillery as part of the agreement. Such weaponry was expensive to operate and the numbers of skilled men to actually fire such weapons would have been difficult to recruit. Known as gunners, any men who may have served with the Welsh would almost certainly have been mercenaries. As such, they would have required payment whether they fired their guns or not, if their loyalty was to be retained. For them it had to be a daily wage because they had to maintain their weapons in good working order, move them from one location to another, all of which required their attentions, and for this they had to be paid.

Early artillery fired stone projectiles shaped into balls, which would have been propelled at low velocities. The artillery force would have fired only a few times and its accuracy at a distance from a castle would not have allowed

71 A recreated type of light medieval artillery which would have been used during the fifteenth century. It is possible that Glyn Dwr's forces used these kind of weapons, supplied by the French. The English, certainly, were using artillery in battle at this time

such weapons to concentrate their fire at a specific spot. However, when the target was something the size of a castle it did not matter about sustained accuracy to batter the garrison of a castle. If the weapons could create a breach in the walls, that was a bonus and would be exploited. Gunners in Welsh employ with their artillery would have been spread in small units across the army, but their presence would have been a welcome addition to any besieging force *(70)*.

The castle defenders would have dreaded the appearance of artillery which could, under certain circumstances, be moved in close to the walls to batter them more effectively. One preferred method of creating a breach in the walls of a castle was to move the artillery close enough in order that it could concentrate fire against one particular spot on the wall. When the projectiles had sufficiently damaged the section of the wall it would collapse under its own weight. This created the desired breach into which the troops could rush and assault the castle. Unfortunately, there is no conclusive proof, either written or archaeological, to indicate that Glyn Dwr had artillery that could have achieved this result at a castle *(71)*.

Apart from Harlech castle receiving gunpowder artillery for defensive purposes in 1405, we learn that Pembroke castle was receiving a similar supply in preparation for attack. A list of supplies from Brecon, dated February 1404, shows that the English were moving in numbers of these powerful weapons. The inventory lists, among other items, six cannon, 20lbs of gunpowder, 10lbs of sulphur and 20lbs of saltpetre: these last two substances (along with charcoal) are required to make gunpowder. The English also brought a massive weapon, known as a bombard, called 'The Messager' (or possibly 'The Messenger') to help in the retrieval of Aberystwyth castle in 1407. It weighed 5,000lbs and fired at the defences during the siege, which lasted until 1408. Such weapons were prone to exploding on being fired, and so it was with The Messager. It was destroyed when for unknown reasons the great weapon was blown apart, killing several people in the vicinity. The English were capable of bringing in such weapons from Bristol and moving them by sea from Pontefract to Carmarthen. They also had better accessibility to these weapons and could replace them if lost in battle or accidental explosions. Such weaponry was expensive, and the fact that Henry IV was using it in Wales when he could have sent it against the French is a mark of how serious he took this latest rebellion to the west of his kingdom.

During 1403 the Welsh scored a number of victories against the English, taking Carmarthen, which would remain in Welsh possession until 1409, with a force of some 8,000 men and thereby securing most of south Wales. This town on the River Tywi was very important and the English had expended large amounts of money in protecting it from Welsh attack. In the year that it was taken the budget for the garrison to defend the castle was £5,160, which was a considerable sum. In 1403, Glyn Dwr also entered into an alliance with Henry Percy, the first earl of Northumberland, because the Percy family harboured grievances against Henry IV. Under the terms of their alliance the actual military command of the Percy forces in the field would be the responsibility of the earl's son, Sir Henry 'Hotspur' Percy. Some sources say that the Percy family were not so aggrieved as to want to readily join the Welsh in war against the king. Whatever the case may be, the fact remains that Henry 'Hotspur' marched southwards in England with a force of 4,000 men, possibly with the intention of joining forces with the Welsh. The army of King Henry, numbering some 5,000 men, outmanoeuvred the Percy force and on 21 July defeated them at the battle of Shrewsbury. The young Henry 'Hotspur' was killed in the fighting and his father withdrew support, thereby depriving Glyn Dwr of English allies. One result of the short-lived alliance was that it stirred the forces in Flint, which normally gave no cause for concern, to take sides with Glyn Dwr. Whilst he had lost one ally, he had gathered another, proving to the king that he was far from being beaten.

Unperturbed at the defeat of their English ally, the Welsh continued to achieve success against the English and only met failure in their repeated

 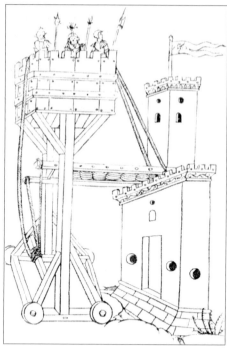

72 Left   Scaling ladders were still in use and were most effective in climbing walls, providing the defenders could be kept from tipping them back

73 Right   Assault towers such as this took time to construct and required carpenters as well as raw materials. Glyn Dwr's forces are recorded as using such devices to attack castles being held by English garrisons. Such structures were stable platforms from which archers could shoot into the ranks of the defenders

attempt to take Caernarfon in November 1403. This was a major blow and Glyn Dwr lost over 300 men in the attack as they tried to storm this very powerful fortress. He tried to take Caernarfon again in 1404, only to be beaten back once more. What is so significant about this second defeat in front of Caernarfon is the fact that despite the castle's massive size the garrison only comprised 28 men. Their success in defending the castle is as much a testimony to their tenacity as to the inherent strength of the castle and its design which made it possible to be held by such a small garrison. A letter dated 16 January 1404 gives us an insight into events at the time:

> The Welsh rebels of Owain Glyn Dwr with the French and all his other forces are preparing to assault the town and castle of Caernarfon. They have begun to do so on the very day we write these letters with engines, siege equipment, and very long ladders. There are only twenty-eight fighting men in the town and castle and that is too small a force. Eleven of the more able men who were there during the last siege have died, some of them from wounds suffered at the time

of the assault, and others of plague. The castle and town are in very great danger
as the bearer of these letters will testify to you by word of mouth.

The letter was apparently carried by a woman because no man could be spared
or found who was brave enough for the duty. This communication, however,
tells us something of Glyn Dwr's siege equipment. It appears that he was still
relying on traditional methods such as scaling ladders, catapults and possibly
battering rams to pound the doors and walls *(72)*. There is no mention of
gunpowder weapons, but it may be that the correspondent was making passing
reference to 'engines', or had not identified them at the time of writing *(73)*.

The Welsh had suffered some defeats on the battlefield in 1403, but in
addition, their homesteads were being reduced by the English in an effort to
prevent the settlements from providing food to the rebels. The war was costing
England dearly and draining the war chest, which could have otherwise been
spent in fighting the French. For example, a combined garrison strength of
1,415 men was deployed to sixteen castles costing a daily rate of £42. The war
was proving costly in money and men, and the king was desperate for a
solution to be brought about.

But despite this, not all was going badly for the Welsh in 1403, because a
number of castles were attacked and taken, or declared their intention to
support Glyn Dwr. At Dryslwyn, for example, the commander of the
garrison, Rhys ap Gruffydd, sided with the Welsh prince and the castle was
used as a base of operations from where attacks could be launched on other
castles in the area, including Kidwelly, Carreg Cennen, Llandovery and
Llanstephan. Garrisons were being increased and supplied in readiness to fight
off attacks by the Welsh. For example it was Henry IV himself who, in 1403,
directed that Manorbier castle be placed in a defensible state in preparation
for attack by Owain Glyn Dwr *(74)*. This was not the only castle to receive
this direct order from the king. At Laugharne the constable, Henry Lestrope,
was instructed to prepare the castle and place it in good order should it be
attacked by Owain Glyn Dwr. Other castles to be attacked in 1403 included
Dinefwr, where on 7 July the constable composed a letter, 'writing in haste
and in dread', because he believed he would have no option other than to
abandon the castle under cover of darkness and fall back on Brecon. In the
event, the castle was badly damaged during the siege but not captured.
Haverfordwest also withstood the attentions of the Welsh, not yielding to
their attacks. The siege at Carreg Cennen castle caused considerable damage,
in fact thirteen years after the attack of 1403, a document refers to the walls
being repaired after 'lately [being] completely destroyed and thrown down by
the rebels'. The castle had been held by the constable, John Skydmore
(sometimes written as John Scudamore) who during the attack had pleaded
with the Welsh to allow safe passage for his wife and her mother. His request
was ignored and the castle fell after it was badly damaged. Carreg Cennen

74 Manorbier castle the birthplace of Geraldus Cambrensis (Gerald of Wales) was placed in a state of readiness to withstand possible attack by Glyn Dwr. It appears to have escaped the full attentions of Glyn Dwr's forces

would be repaired and take a small part in the later Wars of the Roses in the struggle for monarchy of England.

When Owain Glyn Dwr marched down the Tywi valley, where Carreg Cennen castle is located on a rocky outcrop overlooking the River Loughor, in 1403 he was leading a force estimated at a strength of 8,000 men, which supports the theory that he was able to raise a considerable army and put it into the field against the English. He was moving down from Brecon and initially it looked like he was going to bypass the castle. Instead he moved to invest it in a siege operation. John Skydmore wrote a letter to the receiver at Brecon on 5 July 1403 in which he details events in the area:

> Worshipful Sir, I recommend me to you, and forasmuch as I may not spare no man from this place away from me, to certify neither the king, not my lord the prince of the mischief of these countries about, nor no man may pass by no way hence, I pray you and require you that ye certify them how all Carmarthenshire, Kidwelly, Carnwaltham [Carnwyllion] and Ys Kennen be sworn to Owen yesterday, and he lay last night in the castle of Drosselan [Dryslwyn] with Rees ap Griffith: and there I was and spake with him upon truce, and prayed of a safe conduct, under his seal, to send home my wife and her mother, and their company, and he would none grant me; and on this day he is about the town of Carmarthen, and there thinketh to abide till he have

the town and castle; and his purpose is from thence into Pembrokeshire, for he holds him sure of all the castles and towns in Kidwelly, Gowerland and Glamorgan, for the same countries have undertaken the sieges of them until they be won. Wherefore write to Sir Hugh Waterton, and to all that ye suppose will take this matter to heart, that they excite the king hitherwards in all haste, to avenge him on some of his false traitors the which he has overmuch cherished, and rescue the towns and castles in these countries, for I dread full sure there be too few true men in them. I can no more as now; but pray God help you and us that think to be true. Written at the castle of Carreg Cennen ye 5th day of July.

This was an impassioned plea for assistance by anyone, especially the king, but in the end it went unanswered for there were no relief forces to march to the aid of the castle. What the final assault on the castle was like we do not know. However, John Skydmore lived until 1435, which tells us he survived the battle as probably did his wife and her mother. After Glyn Dwr's rebellion ended some £500 was spent on repairing the castle between 1414 and 1421, only for it to be destroyed during the Wars of the Roses.

Glyn Dwr next decided to enter a formal alliance with the French, and in 1404 he entered into negotiations which would see him gaining support from that quarter. In one landing at Milford Haven the French brought ashore some 3,000 troops, including 600 crossbowmen from a fleet of 400 ships, which also brought supplies to Glyn Dwr. According to records, a Welsh force of some 10,000 met them, before moving on to campaign against Picton castle and the fortified town of Tenby. Aberystwyth castle fell to Owain Glyn Dwr's forces when the supply ship *La Laurence*, sailing from Bristol, was captured by Henry Dwnn and William Gwyn, who denied the garrison supplies. The castle at Aberystwyth was besieged by Henry Prince of Wales in 1406, but the garrison, commanded by Rhys Ddu, held out against the bombardment from both gunpowder weapons, catapults and trebuchets. In May 1404 Glyn Dwr wrote to King Charles VI of France and invoked the name of Owain Lawgoch. Like his namesake Owain Lawgoch of the 1370s, he would receive financial support, manpower and equipment. Glyn Dwr continued to campaign and in that year he took three major towns, each with castles, and his forces laid siege to a number of other sites, including Cardigan, which was taken and held until 1405. The English military force was being stretched to its fullest capacity, and engaged in fighting a war on two fronts. Perhaps the strangest part about the Hundred Years War still being fought in France was the fact that the English army contained a great number of Welshmen serving as archers. It was they and their predecessors who had given the English such sterling victories with their prowess in use of the longbow, at battles such as Crécy and Poitiers in 1346 and 1356 respectively. The Welsh had given the English army the longbow, which has been termed the 'first secret weapon' in history. That

75   The French fleet bringing reinforcements and supplies to support Owain Glyn Dwr. The force is seen here approaching Milford Haven in 1405 with much-needed arms, equipment and mercenary troops

is undeniable and the Welsh were true masters in the skill of archery. Nevertheless the loyalties of such men must have been severely stretched.

In 1405 Haverfordwest castle was attacked by Owain Glyn Dwr, and although the outer gate was badly damaged, it withstood the siege. At this particular action the Welsh were joined by a French force of over 2,000 men who were still landing troops and supplies at Milford Haven (75). Despite this numerical superiority the castle still managed to hold out against the powerful attacking force. This was not the first time, however, that the French had supported the Welsh. In 1403 some French seamen had joined Glyn Dwr in attacking Caernarfon and Kidwelly castles, but that was not part of the official military support and may well have been a mercenary force acting independently of the French king. The 1405 campaign with official French support marched to St Clears, captured Carmarthen castle and advanced across the border into England as far as Worcester. Then, for some inexplicable reason Glyn Dwr ordered a withdrawal back to Wales. Possibly he thought he had overstretched his lines of communication and feared being cut off by the English. Following this decision, many of the French troops were re-embarked and sailed back to France.

76   The castle at Grosmont close to where the forces of Owain Glyn Dwr attacked the army commanded by Henry of Monmouth, Prince of Wales. The castle was attacked but held out against the assault and the Welsh were repulsed, taking with them large amounts of supplies from the English camp

At this time Glyn Dwr's forces were engaged in two open battles between March and May. The first battle was fought in March 1405 at Grosmont, north-west of Skenfrith, where a compact but very strong castle lay. Grosmont itself was a very important site, guarding a crossing over the River Monnow and was garrisoned for the king *(76)*. What began as a siege of the castle under Owain Glyn Dwr, turned into a battle when Henry of Monmouth, the Prince of Wales, arrived with a relieving force. He attacked the main Welsh column, led by Rhys Grethin, who were taken by surprise at the suddenness of the assault. It was a much-needed English victory, at a time when there appeared to be nothing but bad news from all the battlefields. In his report to his father the king, Henry of Monmouth related how he faced a force of some 8,000 Welshmen and killed at least 1,000 of Owain Glyn Dwr's men. This may be a slight exaggeration but the fact remains this was a significant victory for the English. What Prince Henry omitted to tell his father was the fact that Owain Glyn Dwr had attacked his baggage train and captured the bulk of his supplies, horses and other valuables including food. Adam of Usk tells how in this action:

And again the same Owain did harm the English considerably, killing many of them, and took the arms, horses and tents of the king's eldest son, the Prince of Wales, and many other lords, to do as he wished with them in the mountain lairs of Snowdonia.

The following month Prince Henry was created lieutenant in north Wales and his force in the field comprised of 500 men-at-arms and 2,000 archers. A further 2,000 troops were placed at various castles to increase the garrisons. Moves were now being made to put pressure on the Welsh and wear them down with superior numbers of troops at strategic locations.

The second major battle of the war was fought on 15 May 1405 at Pwll Melyn, northeast of Usk, where the small but important castle had already been attacked and destroyed by Owain Glyn Dwr. Some sources place the date of this action as being 15 March, but most records point towards 15 May being the most likely date. Owain Glyn Dwr's forces, commanded by his brother Tudur ap Gruffudd (sometimes referred to as Tudor Glyn Dwr) were positioned at the top of the hill at Pwll Melyn (The Yellow Pool) when the English charged. Attacking uphill is usually an ill-advised manoeuvre, but on this occasion the tactic proved successful and the Welsh were defeated. In the fighting Tudur was killed and Owain Glyn Dwr's son, Gruffudd, was captured along with some 300 other Welshmen. All the prisoners were executed at Penffald, with the exception of Gruffudd who was taken to London and for the remainder of his life kept prisoner, variously in the Tower of London and Nottingham castle. Among those others killed in the battle was John ap Hywel, the abbot of Llantarnam, which lay near Caerleon. It was terrible loss which the Welsh could ill afford

The English had at last gained a great victory and the Welsh were sorely weakened by such losses. There were also some Welshmen leading their own retinue against Glyn Dwr, such as Dafydd Gam, who had also been present at Grosmont and as a member of the *uchelwyr* was a powerful figure from a wealthy and well-respected family. The myth of Owain Glyn Dwr's supposed invincibility was beginning to be shattered as the English mounted an aggressive offensive into the country, driving the Welsh garrisons out of those castles being held for Glyn Dwr. One by one these castles were reclaimed until finally only Harlech remained as the last great castle being garrisoned in his name. Finally this site, too, was recaptured by the English who also seized Glyn Dwr's wife and other family, including his three granddaughters. The Welsh garrison had been particularly obstinate in their defence of the castle, perhaps because they were protecting the family of their prince and leader.

Aberystwyth castle had surrendered in September 1408 and other castles had been seized by the English. According to the chronicles Aberystwyth was attacked by the besieging force which reduced the castle's defences: 'by mynes and all manner of engines that were thought needful for the distruccion of them and of there castle.' Any losses to the king's forces could be made good, and despite the wars in France the crown could always send weapons and supplies to continue the war against Glyn Dwr's forces. The Welsh on the other hand did not have access to reinforcements and replacement supplies and weapons. In October 1406 the French had withdrawn their support for Glyn Dwr, leaving him with ever-diminishing prospects of continuing the war. The loss of Harlech castle was too much for him and he had no other option but to withdraw back into the hills where he knew the English would not dare follow.

He was accompanied by several of his most trusted aides including Gruffudd Young, Philip Hanmer and the brothers Gwilym and Rhys ap Tudur ap Goronwy. From the secure remoteness this band of desperate men continued to mount sporadic attacks against the English. These were more akin to nuisance raids and were more likely to provoke reprisal actions by the English against any of the local populace suspected of giving aid to the rebels. The man once feared by friend and foe alike was now reduced to a fugitive-like figure, not unlike that of Vortigen nearly 1,000 years earlier. The great war leader was now an exile in his own country and being hunted by a ruthless enemy. Glyn Dwr had lost everything, his lands, title, wealth and family, in his war against the English. He was now losing the last vestiges of his dignity and growing ever weaker with each passing month.

By 1413 Glyn Dwr had gone from being an omnipotent commander in battle to a man forced into hiding like a common outlaw. Once, his name had been omnipresent at all castle sieges and battles across Wales and struck fear into his enemies. After 1415, nothing is heard about this once great and enigmatic figure. Some sources claim that he died in September 1415 at the home of one of his daughters, Alys Scudamore, at Monnington in Herefordshire. Among the English he had gained notoriety while in the years after the great rebellion his memory lived on in the history of Wales where he is quite rightly still seen as a great leader in war. Even today, no one is entirely sure as to his final place of burial or the date and cause of his death. A manuscript appeared around 1560, which is believed to be a copy of an earlier record in which reference is made to Glyn Dwr's fate: 'many say that he died; the *brudwyr* [the prophetic poets] say that he did not'. The legend of Owain Glyn Dwr was born. The reason for his fall into obscurity following the collapse of his rebellion is simply that other events overshadowed his twilight years.

In 1413, when Glyn Dwr was sheltering in the hills, Henry IV died and his son Henry Prince of Wales was crowned. He ruled as Henry V and would prove to be a capable and fearless king with great authority. His father, Henry IV, had been a strong king, after all, he had had to fight a war on two fronts: the French and Welsh. The historian Ralph A. Griffiths claims that it was the perseverance of Henry IV: 'his decisiveness and readiness to live in the saddle, as he pursued his enemies across England and Wales and to Edinburgh and beyond…', which allowed his son to inherit a unified and peaceful country. Indeed, with his kingdom at peace with itself, Henry V could concentrate on campaigning against the French. On 21 October 1415 he met the French in battle at the site of Agincourt. With a force of about 5,700 men, mostly archers, he confronted a French army of at least 25,000 men, including cavalry. Many of his archers were from Wales, who were proficient in the use of the dreaded longbow. The French army included many Welshmen who were serving as mercenaries. It was not the first time that Welshmen had faced one another across the battlefield, nor would it be the last.

The battle was fiercely fought and very bloody. The English archers shot a deadly storm of arrows into the French cavalry as they repeatedly charged against Henry's positions. The field was very muddy and the withering accuracy of each arrow inflicted heavy losses amongst the 'very flower of French chivalry'. The battle ended with a victory that greatly raised morale within the English ranks and back at home in the court. The French had lost over 5,000 men mainly due to the archers, and another 1,000 were taken prisoner. The king had lost only 400 men and he had reaffirmed his territories in France. It was this news which almost certainly took priority over the death of Owain Glyn Dwr, had it been announced. However, rather than capitalising on his success Henry withdrew rather than risk losing his hard-won gains. The wars in France would continue until 1453, by which time Henry VI was king. The Hundred Years War was finally won by the French when they displaced the English from the country. Thousands of Welshmen had fought and died in the various campaigns during the 116 years of warring, serving mainly as archers on both sides. The war had deprived Wales of men and money and in doing so had prevented economic growth and stability. With peace many hoped that this would be about to change.

In the years following Owain Glyn Dwr's disappearance and other dramatic events the Welsh settled into a period of slow but sure recovery, having been at war for so long. Castles were still garrisoned to maintain the peace across the land and laws were enforced. Those smaller, less important, castles were neglected and allowed to fall into disuse, to be forgotten about over a period of time. The larger sites were improved, repaired and maintained, for they stood as the symbol of power across the land, in the same way as the first Norman castles had almost four centuries earlier. There was minor in-fighting between rival families but nothing so serious that it warranted royal intervention. After so many years of fighting, it appeared to most that with the end of the Hundred Years War in 1453 some semblance of normality could return at last to the country. However, it was not to be, because within two years Wales and its great castles would be involved in yet another war.

THE WARS OF THE ROSES: 1455–1485

In early 1455, the House of York and the House of Lancaster declared war on one another in what was essentially a war of dynastic claims. England would virtually tear itself apart in this long, drawn-out civil war. Although none of the major battles in this conflict, which would last thirty years, was fought in Wales, the great castles would be held variously for one side or the other in the dispute for the throne of England. The period has come to be known as the Wars of the Roses, due to the fact that each side used this flower as a symbol of livery. For the Lancastrians the colour of the rose was red whilst the House of York adopted the white rose.

The war was to last until 1485, but it has been calculated that the time actually spent fighting amounted to only thirteen weeks. Wales was to figure in the war because both sides had powerbases in the country and each relied heavily on the country to provide troops. The large-scale battles fought in other parts of the country would be of great interest to the Welsh. The castles would once again figure prominently in yet another war, which would once more see Welshmen fighting Welshmen across the battlefield.

The opposing sides in this complicated series of battles relied heavily on recruiting Welsh troops to their cause. The House of York, for example, raised troops from the earldom of the March and Glamorgan. The Lancastrians depended on Pembroke and the principality to provide loyal troops. The various battles had a profound impact on the country, and as John Davies in his book *A History of Wales* states: 'These battles were of great interest to the Welsh.' They were also a great drain on the country's economy and other resources, including manpower. After the battle of Banbury, the Welshman Lewys Glyn Cothi regarded the huge loss of Welshmen to be disastrous for the country. As an indication of the volume of Welshmen caught up in the fighting, at the battle of Bosworth fought on 22 August 1485, Henry Tudor's force of 5,000 comprised at least one-third Welshmen, the remainder being some 3,000 Frenchmen. Here then, were examples of Welshmen still fighting in the pay of English kings, whilst Welsh claimants to the throne were still using French mercenaries.

The first full battle of the Wars of the Roses was fought on 22 May 1455 at St Albans, where a force of 3,000 troops led by Richard of York and Warwick defeated a force of 2,000 Lancastrians led by the duke of Somerset. It was a decisive victory for the Yorkists, who captured Henry VI, and Richard proclaimed himself constable of England. Over the next three decades many practices would bring into doubt the notion that the fifteenth century ever had a code of chivalry or any honour. Treason was common, so too was kidnapping and ransom. Murder was more widespread than commonly thought and alliances would be entered into which would set friends against one another. It was a time, in other words, when no one could be trusted.

77   Harlech castle, which was the backdrop to so many actions, including being besieged by the English in 1408. It also played a significant role during the Wars of the Roses

The fighting between the two royal factions only approached the Welsh border in 1459, after the Yorkist victory at the battle of Blore Heath on 3 September that year. Various engagements continued until the Yorkists defeated the Lancastrians once more, this time at the battle of Mortimer's Cross, 2 February 1461, and the victorious prince took the crown to rule as Edward IV. The matter of eliminating any remaining Lancastrian resistance in south Wales was entrusted to William Herbert, who had been elected as justiciar for life in 1461. He was later elected to the same post in north Wales in 1467 after the fall of the towns of Tenby and Pembroke. Jasper Tudor, who was loyal to the House of Lancaster and Henry VI, was stripped of his titles and forced to flee to safety in Ireland.

In 1468 Jasper Tudor returned to north Wales and began attacking various points, including Denbigh castle, which was held by a determined garrison. Not being equipped with the weaponry to assault the strong defences of the castle, Jasper could only burn the town. William Herbert went into action and mounted a strong campaign. Together with his brother, Sir Richard Herbert, he attacked Harlech castle, which was being held for the Lancastrians by a garrison commanded by Sir Daffydd ap Ieuan ab Einion (sometimes referred to as Sir David ap Jevan ap Einion). This was the last bastion holding out for the otherwise lost Lancastrian cause. The chronicler John Warkworth wrote:

> Kyng Edward was possessed of alle Englonde, excepte a castelle in Northe
> Wales called Harlake, which Sere Richard Tunstall kepte, the the qwiche was
> gotene afterwards by the Lord Harbede.

This was really Lord William Herbert of Raglan, whom Edward IV would
later in 1468 create Lord Pembroke, which had been Jasper Tudor's title, in
recognition for services rendered.

Edward had instructed Lord William to seize Harlech castle, for which task
a besieging force of between 7,000 and 10,000 men were raised. The two
brothers marched on the powerful castle with its commanding position and
invested it in a siege, which was to last for nearly one month. The writings of
Hywel Dafi relate the conduct of the siege and tell how the attackers were
'shattered by the sound of guns' with 'seven thousand men shooting in every
port, their bows made from every yew tree'. Completely surrounded and with
no hope of a relief force, the Lancastrians, reduced to a strength of only fifty
men, had no other option but to surrender. Among those taken captive was
Daffydd ap Ieuan ab Einion, who had so valiantly strived to keep 'little Harlech
for so long, alone faithful to the weak crown'. This commander was no
stranger to warfare and is alleged to have said that:

> he had once in his youth maintained a castle so long in France that every old
> woman in Wales had heard of it, and in his old age had held a castle in Wales
> for so long that every old woman in France had heard of it.

Other Welsh castles were fought over during this stage of the Wars of the
Roses, and the fate of the country was still far from settled. Carmarthen castle,
for example, was seized by a Lancastrian force led by Henry and Morgan ap
Thomas, but with support for their cause not forthcoming they were obliged
to relinquish the site. Sir William Herbert was the first Welshman to be
ennobled by an English king and his power in the land was unquestioned. One
poet of the time wrote of him as being 'King Edward's master-lock'. In 1468,
flushed with his success at Harlech castle he was seen by many as the king's
man, but deep down he was a troubled man and not settled with the state of
affairs in the country *(77)*. It would be another poet, Guto'r Glyn, who
enjoyed high position in court and was pleased in the 'wearing of the fine
collar of the guard and the livery of king Edward', who would ultimately prove
the undoing of Sir William Herbert. It was Guto'r Glyn who urged him to
take up the cause and expel the English and unite Wales.

However, Sir William Herbert had enemies in very powerful circles, one of
whom was the earl of Warwick, who envied the power held by this Welshman.
The king trusted him and within Wales he was respected, but at the same time
in England he was feared. He was ruthless in war and reliable to his king. These
were attributes, which further alienated him to his English counterparts who

could not understand such sentiments. Matters finally came to a head in 1469
when the earl of Warwick rebelled against Edward IV and sought the restoration of Henry VI, who had been deposed in 1461. On the morning of 26 July
Sir William Herbert and his brother Richard found themselves facing the earl
of Warwick across the battlefield at Edgecote, close to Banbury. The engagement that followed was a relatively minor battle in the Wars of the Roses, but
the consequences would be felt for a long time. The battle appeared, at first,
to be going in favour of the Welshmen who broke through Warwick's lines and
it seemed that they had won the action. Suddenly to their rear appeared a body
of troops, which Sir William believed to be the earl of Stafford arriving in his
support. He could not have been taken by greater surprise when it became
apparent that it was another body of Warwick's forces. The Welsh forces
collapsed and began to run from the field. They were hacked to pieces as they
attempted to flee from the newly arrived troops. Sir William and his brother
were taken prisoner and transported to Northampton, where they were both
executed on the 27 July on the orders of Warwick himself. Sir William's place
at court was taken by Richard, duke of Gloucester, King Edward's brother. His
allegiance had never been put to the test when it came to the question of
Wales, and it will never been known, whether or not Sir William would have
risen in revolt as Owain Glyn Dwr had done, and to whom he has often been
compared.

Wales, with no popular local leader, was thrown into turmoil. Further
fighting continued but the most powerful castles in Wales were now garrisoned
for Yorkists and any hope of an uprising was becoming increasingly less likely.
The battle of Tewkesbury, 2 June 1471, produced yet another Yorkist victory,
but this time the Lancastrians paid a severe price for defeat. Edward, Prince of
Wales, who had commanded the Lancastrian forces, was taken prisoner along
with the earl of Somerset, and executed. When Henry VI was murdered in
1471, Edward IV was king of his realm and the House of York were victorious.
It has been argued that Tewkesbury was the single most important battle
regarding Wales to be fought during the Wars of the Roses, presumably
because the lineage for Lancastrian heir to the throne had been wiped out.
Jasper Tudor, uncle to the murdered Henry VI sailed to Brittany in France,
taking with him his nephew Henry, the son of Edmund Tudor, who had died
in 1456. It was a significant saving of life, because all hopes of the Lancastrian
cause now rested on the fate of these exiles. Jasper realised it was too late to
save Henry VI but he could at least preserve the lineage of the dynasty. Edward
IV declared Henry Tudor: 'was the only imp now left of Henry VI's brood.'
But this 'imp' was to return and wreak a vengeance which would found a
powerful dynasty.

Henry Tudor had been born after the death of his father and raised by Sir
William Herbert of Raglan. When Sir William was executed, Jasper Tudor, as
his uncle, took up the mantle and raised the young boy. Jasper was more than

just a guardian, he was also the figurehead for the Lancastrian cause in Wales. The rescue of his ward as they sailed into exile was not without its dangers. As they approached the coast of France they were shipwrecked and compelled to reside as reluctant guests of Francis Duke of Brittany. In effect they were prisoners, but granted privileges according to their status as nobles. In fact, Jasper Tudor was known to travel to Wales on several occasions for meetings with various figures.

An astute man, Jasper must have realised that Edward IV would not reign forever. His visits put him in contact with powerful Welshmen such as Sir John Dwnn of Kidwelly, this being the site of a powerful castle on the mouth of the River Tywi. This allowed him to sail directly from France to conduct clandestine meetings. Others with whom he was familiar included Gruffydd Dwnn, Sir Richard Gethin and Matthew Gough, all soldiers with much experience in military affairs. This state of affairs was to last for over thirteen years, and all the while plots and schemes were being hatched. Most of these came to nought, but in 1483 everything changed when Edward IV died in April 1483, leaving his son Edward as heir. He was challenged by his uncle, Richard, who seized the crown from the young twelve-year-old prince. The country once more faced civil war.

With this avaricious act he declared himself Richard III and usurped Edward, who had been declared Prince of Wales, and would otherwise rule as King Edward V. The toppled boy king was taken to the Tower of London, along with his brother Richard. They were both put to death, most likely on the orders of their uncle Richard. He wasted no time and set about negotiating with the duke of Brittany to have Jasper Tudor and his ward Henry sent to another part of France. No doubt some part where they would find it more difficult to have access to the sea routes connecting to Wales. But, his schemes went badly awry when they relocated just at the time that France was planning to attack England.

Richard had declared his son Edward as Prince of Wales, but the boy died in 1484. He was facing a crisis in his reign and he was not proving a popular king as events appeared to be once more spiralling towards civil war. In France, uncle and nephew believed the time was right for action and with French support set sail at the head of an invasion fleet composed of French mercenaries and Welsh exiles. In the meantime Richard had been trying to create reliable supporters and had entrusted various castles in Wales to personages on whom he thought he could depend. One of these was Richard Williams, to whom he entrusted Manorbier castle and several other castles with a view to protecting the coast of Wales from attack, which might come from the direction of Milford Haven. It was almost as if Richard had had a premonition. Pembroke castle was repaired, as were a number of other sites that had been allowed to fall into disrepair.

On 1 August 1485 Henry Tudor and his uncle set sail from Harfleur with a force of some 3,000 troops *(78)*. They made landfall at Dale in Mill Bay by

78 Henry Tudor, who reigned as King
Henry VII. He founded a dynasty which
ruled England and Wales for 116 years

Milford Haven on 7 August, where Jasper was greeted with the words:
'Welcome! For thou hast taken good care of thy nephew'. Although the
returning exiles were greeted with cordiality there was no great rush to join
their ranks. On the other hand, there was no resistance as over the coming
week they marched across the land trying to gather supporters for their cause,
which was to depose the despised Richard III and the House of York. As the
Lancastrian army moved further into Wales they gained support from such
figures as Rhys ap Thomas of Dinefwr, who had been in correspondence with
Henry whilst in France. Rhys joined Henry's force, bringing with him a large
body of men, having been induced to support the cause when promised the

government of Wales if the campaign was successful. Others rallied to his banner and when Henry's army reached Newport he was joined by Sir Gilbert Talbot and Sir John Savage, who had a combined following of 2,000 men, which brought the force up to a strength of about 6,000 troops.

The Tudors, both Jasper and Henry, had a direct association with Pembroke, where one of the most powerful castles dominated the surrounding lands. Jasper had been dispossessed of his title as earl of Pembroke after the Yorkist victory at the battle of Towton on 29 March 1461. He had been granted the castle and his titles by dint of the fact that he was the half-brother of Henry VI. His father was Owain Tudor, a Welsh squire descended from the twelfth-century Welsh prince Rhys ap Gruffudd, who had married Queen Catherine of Valois in France, the widow of Henry V. As a result of this marriage they had three sons, Edmund, Jasper and Owen, who followed different paths in life and met with equally different fates. Owain Tudor was not just an opportunist, he had served the crown with commendable loyalty in France and England, and was highly regarded and trusted at court. Indeed, his loyalty would cost him his life, when he was executed after the battle of Mortimer's Cross on 2 February 1461. During her marriage to Henry V, Catherine had given birth to a son, the future king, Henry VI, thus her three sons resulting from her marriage to Owain Tudor became the king's half-brothers. There was no animosity between the men and Edmund was created earl of Richmond by his half-brother, Henry VI. Edmund married Margaret Beaufort, who was descended from John of Gaunt, died in 1456 and his son, Henry Tudor, was born posthumously in Pembroke castle in 1457. Owen entered the church and became a monk, eventually dying in 1501 without ever having entered marriage.

This left Jasper, who being stripped of his titles and Pembroke castle, which was granted to William Herbert by Edward IV in 1461, was virtually alone in a hostile country. When the Lancastrian army was defeated at the battle of Barnet on 14 April 1471, Jasper retreated into the castle, where he was briefly besieged. The castle at Pembroke was now integral to the survival of the Tudor lineage. It was from here that Jasper fled with his ward Henry Tudor into exile in France. Henry was the last claimant to the throne, but only descended by the most tenuous of links through his grandmother.

THE BATTLE OF BOSWORTH AND THE RISE OF THE TUDORS

Nevertheless, Henry Tudor had a right to challenge the throne of England and continued his march across Wales towards Shrewsbury and England. He crossed the River Severn at Shrewsbury, all the while gaining support. Richard III was not slow to respond to this threat and advanced with an army towards Leicester. He sent out messengers to summon his lords, including the duke of Norfolk,

79 The battle of Bosworth, 21 August 1485, the final battle in the Wars of the Roses. Here, Richard III fights for his life at the crucial point of the battle. Henry Tudor was victorious and provided the country with its first king of Welsh lineage

Lord Stanley, earl of Northumberland and Lord Lovell from London, along with Brackenbury from Hampshire. Of these supporters for the king, only Stanley refused to rally to the king's summons, stating that he was too ill to join the fight. Richard was furious at this and threatened to execute Lord Strange, the son of the errant earl. Lord Strange immediately made to abscond but was seized, whereupon he confessed that he and his uncle, Sir William Stanley, chamberlain of north Wales, had agreed to join the forces of Henry Tudor.

On the morning of 21 August 1485 Richard moved his camp to within two miles of Bosworth. His army now numbered between 10,000 and 11,000 men, including mounted troops and archers *(79)*. Henry was also approaching the same area and his force had grown to about 7,000, including mounted troops, men-at-arms and also a body of archers. Following a night camped on the edges of the battlefield the two sides took up positions on 22 August, with Richard's army greatly outnumbering that of Henry Tudor. Richard also had the advantage of controlling the highest point on the field, Ambion Hill, from where he could observe everything. In fact, it was from this position that he spied a small party separated from the main army, in which was Henry. Being impetuous Richard charged down to engage the group. However, he became bogged down in the muddy ground and the force of the Stanleys, who until that point had played no part in the battle, moved forward and cut Richard's unit to pieces and killed the king.

The battle was won and Henry Tudor was recognised as king. The Stanley family were now regarded as 'the king makers', but only through their hesitating to join battle until the most opportune moment. Once the most propitious time had been identified to commit themselves, the Stanley family seized on the moment and changed the course of the battle. The exact number of casualties inflicted on the House of York varies between 1,000 and 4,000, but it was the death of Richard which decided the outcome of the battle. Henry as the victorious head of the House of Lancaster rode into nearby Leicester and was proclaimed king. It was as though the old Welsh prophecies concerning the mythical figure of Merlin from the court of the legendary Camelot and King Arthur had come true. During the reign of Edward II, 1327–1377, a chronicler had recorded:

> At one time the Welsh were noble and had sovereignty over the whole of England... And according the sayings of the prophet Merlin they will one day repossess England. Thus the Welsh frequently revolt in the hope of fulfilling the prophecy; but as they know not the hour, they are often deceived and their labour is in vain.

It certainly looked as if the cycle of history had indeed come full circle and the Welsh were once again masters of the country, which had been theirs almost 1,000 years earlier. The Venetian ambassador to England at the time of the battle of Bosworth wrote of the outcome: 'The Welsh may now be said to have recovered their former independence, for the wise and fortunate Henry VII is a Welshman.' The poet Dafydd Llwyd of Mathafarn near Machynlleth, the site of Owain Glyn Dwr's parliament, had sung of the return of Jasper Tudor as early as 1468. Like the fabled prophesies of Merlin, Dafydd had predicted how: 'The brave, long haired exile will come with his mansions riding the salt water.' However, not all Welshmen accepted Henry VII, and the historian John Davies argues in his book, *A History of Wales*, that: 'It was not a matter of the Tudors identifying themselves with the Welsh but rather the Welsh identifying themselves with the Tudors.' Within the court at London there was no great affection towards Wales. According to some researchers Henry VII was one-half English, one-quarter French and only one-quarter Welsh. But for many that was sufficient to claim the dynasty now founded under the Tudors was as had been foretold. The dynasty of the Tudors would last for 118 years and withstand many tribulations.

One of the first challenges to the reign of Henry VII came at the battle of Stoke Field on 16 June 1487, when Lord Lovell and Robert de la Pole, earl of Lincoln, supported a pretender to the throne – ten-year-old Lambert Simnel, claiming to be a surviving prince from the Tower of London. Henry with a force of 12,000 troops, which included forces led by Sir Rhys ap Thomas of Carew castle, had little or no trouble in defeating an inferior force and either killed or captured the conspirators. He was popular and had proven himself strong in battle and decisive in action. These traits alone doomed to failure any would-be attempt to dethrone him and there was never any support to depose this king.

Henry VII married Elizabeth of York, thus uniting the two royal houses which had fought one another during the Wars of the Roses. From this union they had four children: Prince Arthur in 1486, Margaret in 1489, Prince Henry in 1491 and Mary in 1496. In 1489, at the age of three years, Arthur was proclaimed Prince of Wales, thereby maintaining a tradition of promoting the king's eldest son to this position which dated back to when Henry III proclaimed the future Edward I to the title. In 1490 the council of the new Prince of Wales was being supervised by his great uncle, the all-wise Jasper Tudor. In 1495 Jasper died and other Welshmen were elevated to high positions, such as Rhys ap Thomas, who was knighted in 1496 and created justiciar of south Wales. In 1502, tragedy struck when young Prince Arthur died in his sixteenth year, leaving behind an equally young widow Catherine of Aragon. Two years later, in 1504, Henry VII created his surviving son, the future Henry VIII, as Prince of Wales.

With peace upon the land, it appeared that the country would increase its wealth. Indeed, Henry VII benefited from the discoveries made by the explorations of John Cabot sailing in the *Matthew*. England's wealth was growing and tensions with Wales were now almost a thing of the past. In fact, so good were relations between the two countries that Sir Rhys ap Thomas organised a great tournament in the grounds of his castle at Carew in Pembrokeshire to mark the reconciliation between England and Wales and also to celebrate his being created a Knight of the Order of the Garter. The great gathering was held over a period of six days and was attended by 600 knights. Naturally there was much feasting, but it was also an opportunity for these nobles to show off their prowess in bouts of jousting and other personal displays of skill at arms. Castles across Wales were being transformed into grand houses, where the owners lived in great opulence and decorated the halls with tapestries and furnishings. Elsewhere, the smaller castles, of lesser importance and of little or no strategic value were allowed to crumble into decay and were even plundered by the local populace for building materials. For all intents and purposes the age of the castle and the reason for their very being was long gone, to be replaced by comfort instead of functionality. However, events were to prove such believers wrong and efforts were made to redress the decline of Welsh castles in their state of preparedness for wars.

6

THE CIVIL WAR
AND BEYOND

By the end of the fifteenth century the importance of the castle, in the form
of that built during the reign of Edward I, was in decline. In fact during the
whole of the fifteenth century no new royal castles were built anywhere, and
especially none in Wales, and there were no licences granted to crenelate, that
is to say build walls with 'battlements', or fortify any manor house. Only the
king could grant such a right, and with no decrees issued it would appear that
military thinkers of the time recognised the fact that the castle was becoming
an anachronism of military doctrines of the day. It has been opined that the
reason for this stems from the increased use of gunpowder weapons on the
battlefield, especially artillery, which was growing ever more powerful. The
late historian and author of several volumes on castles, R. Allen Brown,
believed that the introduction of gunpowder and the development of heavy
cannon had little effect on military architecture. This theory is also held by
Brian K. Davison, an historian on the subject of castles. However, on exami-
nation of the facts, one has to disagree with them because of several factors,
not the least of which was the emerging military trends of the day, especially
that appertaining to fortification.

With the advent of gunpowder artillery and its ever-increasing power, the
natural reaction for architects was to make the walls of castles much thicker in
order to withstand the impact of a stone or iron projectile. However, the design
of these fortifications was never intended as a countermeasure against scientific
approaches to warfare and there was a limit to what could be accomplished
with the many old styles of castles. Over a period of 200 years the walls of the
new fortifications had evolved to be built in a squat style to present targets of
low silhouette, which was less obvious and therefore less vulnerable to attack
by artillery. These new defensive fortifications incorporated their own range of
artillery in their weaponry and were known as artillery forts, some of which
accommodated very powerful cannon.

The decline of traditional castles was, therefore, a gradual process. The occupants of those old-fashioned castles were also changing in their ways of thinking and beginning to alter the interiors to make them more comfortable. Many were prepared to sacrifice the reason for the castle in favour of improving their lifestyles, even if it meant ignoring the fabric strength of the castle itself. This trend was happening in several European countries at the same time, including England and Wales. Elsewhere, however, such as in Scotland and Ireland, the castle still remained the traditional symbol of military power.

Those castles not inhabited were allowed to fall into decay and collapse into piles of masonry rubble. This was seized on by the local populaces of villages, which had grown up in the shadows of these castles. In some cases the stones were transported away in cartloads as a ready-made supply of dressed and prepared building material. Other materials, such as lead and wood, were also stripped and greatly prized. The expense of maintaining the traditional castle was becoming prohibitive, even for the most wealthy families, and as a consequence more often than not they took up residence in more modest dwellings on their estates. There were a few who, through prudence, did manage to cling to some vestige of their former glory and lived in the castle proper in comfortable surroundings, albeit somewhat reduced from what their predecessors enjoyed. Some of the occupants in castles across Wales fell into disfavour with the king and had their properties confiscated.

In 1509, Henry VII died leaving his son and heir, who would rule as Henry VIII, a powerful country both militarily and financially *(80)*. Although the new king, would eventually prove his prowess as a strong king both in matters of state and warfare, he would also prove to be fickle and fastidious in personal taste. Former favourites could find themselves arrested, such as happened to Rhys ap Griffith, the grandson of Rhys ap Thomas, who in 1531 was arrested and executed for the crime of treason. The family lands, including Carew castle, were confiscated and seized by the crown. A description of the castle at Carew informs us how the castles in this period were now being transformed into dwellings with defence as a secondary function. The castle is recorded as having: 'a larder house, a kechyn above the same, with half a lofte over and a waye ledyng in to the batilments, and at one corner a little turret.' Carew, it must be admitted had not been distinguished in Welsh wars, but during the seventeenth century it would find itself thrust into siege warfare and battered by the artillery of the Parliamentarian army during the English Civil War. However, all that was in the future, and during the early years of the reign of Henry VIII there was little, if any, thought given to coastal or land defence around Wales.

In 1536, Henry VIII, declared the Act of Union between England and Wales, the introduction of which meant peace between the two countries and that it was no longer considered imperative that the castles be maintained. The Act of Union also saw the abolition of Marcher Lords and their right to war

80 King Henry VIII, son of Henry VII and Prince of Wales before becoming king in 1509. He introduced the Act of Union between England and Wales in 1536, which in effect brought about a peace between the two regions

without the king's authority, and Wales was reorganised to follow the lines of English rule. This was further reflected in the fact that by the end of the sixteenth century the rot had completely set in, with irreparable damage and neglect being recorded at a number of strategically important sites. For example, the state of the castles at Conwy, Caernarfon and Harlech are singled out for special mention in a report from the Crown Surveyors in 1539. They are recorded as being in a very poor state of repair and would be impossible to defend any of the sites for one hour should the Scots or French elect to invade Wales. Even before this inspection, the decay of castle defences in Wales had been recognised, but little, if any, action was taken to prevent the onset of further dereliction. In 1343 William de Emeldon, reported on the state of five castles built during the reign of Edward I and reported that Beaumaris castle on Anglesey had so many defects in its walls, towers and buildings, that he believed in his estimation some £684 6s 8d would be needed to reverse the rot.

In April 1539, 200 years later, Sir Thomas Bulkeley in his report wrote to the king's secretary, Thomas Cromwell stating that:

> The royal castles in north Wales are unfurnished and have neither guns nor powder, nor other artillery, apart from eight or ten small pieces in Bewmares possessed by the writer. Has provided three barrels of gunpowder, some shot, forty bows and forty sheaves of arrows, with as many coats of fence and sallets and splinters, at his own cost; this is inadequate for such a fortress. Conwey, Carn' and Hardlach castles have nothing in them to defend them for one hour. If enemies secure them hit would cost his majestie a hundred thowsand of his pounds and the losse of maymy a man affor' they shuld be gotten again. Anglesey is but a night's sailing from Scotland... Beseeches a couple of gunners and some good ordnance and powder to defend the King's house in Bewmares.

Only four years later, in 1543, another report on Beaumaris castle states that there is 'scarcely a single chamber... Where a man could lie dry.' The fortunes of Beaumaris were hardly in the ascendancy and within the space of only seventy-five years it was declared in 1609 to be: 'Utterlie decayed'. From these words one can interpret a damning indictment as to the state of the once most powerful castles in the country. It was almost as if in their isolated locations they had been forgotten and neglected, in which case all that money had been spent for nought.

When Henry VIII died in 1547, the throne of England quickly passed through two monarchs, Edward VI, who died in 1553, followed by his half-sister, Mary I, who died in 1558, neither of whom did much for the defence of England or Wales. In 1558 Elizabeth took the throne in what would prove to be the reign of the last Tudor monarch. It would be under her direction that England and Wales regained their status and continued to maintain their defences against would-be invaders. In 1558, England had lost its last possession in France and the country was more vulnerable to invasion than ever before. The perceived threat was seen as coming mainly from France and Spain, and England and Wales now began to construct coastal defences. Some had been started during the reign of Henry VIII and included defences at Dale Point and Angle respectively commanding the north and south landfall approaches leading into Milford Haven. These were in place and armed with artillery at the time of the threat from the Spanish Armada in 1588. With the defeat of this force in July that year by squadrons of the Royal Navy, the coastal defences along the Welsh shoreline were never put to the test. At the time of the Spanish Armada, it had been planned to strengthen Pembroke castle, but in the end it was decided to erect a line of smaller coastal defences to protect Wales from invasion, of which the constructions at Dale and Angle were but two fortifications in the chain. These coastal defences were, in effect, artillery forts and bore no resemblance to the true castle of earlier periods. This was a sign of the times and reflected the scientific approach which was being applied to such purpose-built designs. Artillery towers were stout, low in height and immensely strong as well as being well armed with gunpowder artillery, and these first models were to set the trend for future developments.

But not all defences around Wales were so well prepared. At Caerphilly, for example, the state of the castle was recorded in a report by John Leland (1503–1552). He had conducted an inspection of this site and wrote of it to be nothing more than an impressive ruin. He recorded the state of other sites in the 1530s, and the picture we gain from his notes is that the condition of Caerphilly castle was symptomatic of the pattern throughout Wales. Even Harlech castle, badly battered during the great siege of 1468, had never been subject to a repair programme. No one could have foreseen how important these castles, despite the forlorn state of so many, would prove to be in the events of the 1640s, when they were once more pressed into use as garrisons for troops and fortified for action.

The series of events leading to the outbreak of Civil War in England were deep rooted and complex. In essence, the war was a result of constitutional differences of opinion arising between the king, Charles Stuart, and parliament as to who exactly ruled the country *(81)*. It was obviously only a question of time before such politics spilled over to embroil Wales, Scotland and Ireland, and set the whole kingdom aflame in open warfare.

Initially a number of Welsh members of parliament elected to support the parliamentary cause, but as events deteriorated throughout 1641, they changed their opinions and sided with the king. Thus, when the battle lines were drawn and the first engagements between the forces of the king and parliament were fought in 1642, Wales was largely for the king but there were factions which supported parliament. The area siding most strongly with parliament was Pembroke. More supporters were to be found in other areas such as Chirk, but

81 King Charles I, who had an almost unanimous following in Wales. He failed to hold onto power and as a result was executed as a traitor in 1649

overall with no large supporting movement in the urban areas, the king was able to rely on Wales to supply men, provisions and money for his cause. The exact numbers of Welshmen serving King Charles is difficult to compute, but Welshmen serving in infantry units at the battle of Naseby, 14 June 1645, may have numbered as many as 3,000 levies commanded by Sir Charles Gerrard, who had led them from Wales. The king's army suffered a heavy defeat at this engagement, with many Welshmen being killed.

The first actions of the Civil War to be fought in Wales were confined to those areas where support for the Parliamentarian cause was greatest. This was largely in the south-west part of the country, such as Pembroke, where the castle was reinforced by Parliamentarian troops in 1645. In 1643 the Royalists seized Tenby and Haverfordwest, actions which were followed up in 1644 when the king's men took Cardigan and Carmarthen, to place most of the country under their military control. Parliamentarian forces were not idle but were experiencing mixed fortunes. In June 1644 they captured Oswestry, raiding into Welshpool in August, and followed this by investing Montgomery castle on 4 September 1644.

Montgomery castle had declined in its status from being considered a frontline castle in the fifteenth century, at which time it was held by the Mortimer family. The castle had been transformed into a domestic residence with buildings being used for comfort rather than military occupancy. In 1622 ownership of the castle was transferred to Lord Herbert, who had a brick house built in the middle ward and defences were not deemed to be of any great importance. The result may have been different had Lord Herbert been farsighted enough to see that a political crisis of a kind never before seen in the country was developing between king and parliament. On the morning of 4 September 1644, Lord Herbert, who sided with King Charles and had established a garrison, was stunned to discover that his castle was being invested by a mixed force of cavalry and infantry numbering some 800 men, under the command of Sir Thomas Middleton (sometimes written as Myddleton).

Rather than fight, Lord Herbert entered into negotiations whereby he agreed to pay a ransom, which would guarantee him and his retinue safe passage from the castle. Under the terms he also agreed to discharge his garrison. The Parliamentarians may have not believed Herbert's intentions and on 5 September a small force, under the command of Lieutenant-Colonel James Till, approached the castle gates with an explosive device called a petard. This was a specially developed weapon designed to be placed directly against the gates of a castle in order to destroy them with the blast. Seeing this action, Herbert demanded that they withdraw in accordance with the terms earlier discussed. Petards were not always reliable, but the threat of one such device being used against the gates of Montgomery castle was enough to spread unrest throughout the garrison. They knew that once the gates had been destroyed there would not be much to prevent the castle from being captured.

Despite being asked to withdraw, the detachment armed with the petard stood firm. Sir Thomas Middleton then ordered them to withdraw and agreed that discussions between himself and Lord Herbert would continue on the morning of 6 September. On that day Middleton acknowledged the fact that Herbert was not recognised as a staunch supporter of the king 'and has done nothing to offend Parliament'. Herbert was permitted to keep his land and property, but he should evacuate the castle from where he was given safe conduct to travel to London, where he would retire.

Montgomery had fallen to Parliamentary forces without a shot being fired. However, the castle was counter-attacked by a Royalist force, who now reversed the situation on Middleton. Relief was not long in coming, and on 18 September the Royalist attackers were routed with 400 men being killed in the fighting and a further 1,400 being taken prisoner. According to records of 1644, the 'Certificate of the losses of Lord Herbert and the Inhabitants of the Town of Mountgomery upon the Surrender of Mountgomery Castle' was costly in financial terms. The siege had cost Herbert £4,940 14s and the people of Montgomery town had lost property to the value of £3,066 12s 10d. The castle was slighted after the action and finally demolished in 1644.

Middleton continued to campaign for Parliament, and even invested his own castle at Chirk and campaigned in North Wales. Over the following month the Parliamentarians seized Powys in a daring night attack. It was now evident that the castles in Wales could serve as strongholds for troops loyal to whichever side. In this respect castles originating many hundreds of years previously were once again thrust into the frontline and had to be readied for a war with modern weapons.

82   Chepstow castle, which was subjected to prolonged artillery bombardment in 1645 and 1648. The walls were breached in May 1648 during the second siege and the castle was taken. It was not slighted and was used by the Parliamentarians to house a garrison in the area

Further skirmishing occurred across the country and came to a head at the battle of Colby Heath on 1 August 1645, when the Parliamentary army achieved a full victory. This was followed up on 18 September when Parliamentarians defeated a Royalist force at Montgomery in the largest battle of the Civil War to be fought in Wales. As the Parliamentarians went on the offensive and defeated Royalist forces in open battle, so the support for the king's cause began to wane. This left only the castles controlled by the Royalists.

In May 1648, when Oliver Cromwell arrived in Wales to take charge of operations, Royalist support was all but finished. His first military action in the country came when he ordered troops, under the command of Colonel Ewer, to attack Chepstow on 11 May *(82)*. The opening attacks led to the town being overtaken, but the castle remained in Royalist hands. The garrison was commanded by Sir Nicholas Kemeys, who supported the rebels holding out in Pembroke castle. The walls of Chepstow castle were 9ft thick in places, but on 25 May, it was finally taken when breaches were made by heavy artillery in the area of the walls near the spot called Marten's Tower. A large number of the garrison made good their escape through this gap, but Sir Nicholas was captured and killed by Colonel Ewer's troops. This was not the first time Chepstow had been involved in the fighting of the Civil War. In October 1645 the castle had been held for the king by a garrison of sixty-five men. After a brief siege, the castle had been surrendered and the Parliamentarian forces had captured seventeen pieces of artillery. Following the attack of 1648 Chepstow was not slighted, contrary to the usual practice, and instead was repaired and even strengthened. The curtain walls to the south of the site were thickened and the towers were 'earthed up' to reduce the impact of iron cannonballs. It was probably the only castle to actually be strengthened and, almost unheard of, a garrison was installed in the castle. This made Chepstow a unique site during the Civil War and a permanent garrison remained stationed in the castle until 1690.

Sporadic fighting continued across the country until King Charles was executed in London in January 1649. By then most of the castles had fallen to Parliamentarian forces, with a number of slightings and several being completely destroyed in order to prevent them from being used as centres of future resistance. Among those castles to be slighted were Chirk, Flint, Ruthin, Haverfordwest, Newcastle Emlyn, Caerphilly and Raglan. This last site was actually designated for complete demolition, but its strength was such that it defied the best efforts of labourers equipped with pickaxes and the work was halted. Beaumaris was among a number of other castles destined for slighting, but due to one reason or another the orders were never carried out and the castles were not damaged. In the more dramatic cases the castles were completely and systematically demolished. Abergavenny castle, for example, was ordered to be destroyed by King Charles in 1645, when it was feared it might be captured by Scottish forces and held for parliament. Among those destroyed by Parliamentary forces was the castle at Llandovery, the demolition

83 Caernarfon castle was considered to be so well fortified that it would not fall in the Civil War. It fell to the Parliamentarians and in 1660 was ordered to be demolished, but the work was never started

of which was personally overseen by Oliver Cromwell. The castle at Montgomery was demolished by a labour force of 180 men in 1649, for which they were paid a total of some £600 for the work. In September that same year Aberystwyth castle was blown up by Lieutenant-Colonel Dawking and Captain Barbour, after which the locals moved in to remove the stone for use as building material.

In the years following the report on its decay in 1539, it appears that Caernarfon castle was the subject of a refurbishment programme *(83)*. In fact, so much so was it fortified, that in 1650 it was sufficient to greatly impress the commentator John Taylor. He wrote:

> I thought to have seen a town and a castle, or a castle and town: but I saw both to be one, and one to be both: for indeed a man can hardly divide them in judgement or apprehension: and I have seen many gallant fabrics and fortifications but for compactness and completeness of Caernarvon I never yet saw a parallel. And it is by art and nature so well fitted and seated that it stands impregnable; and if it be well manned, victualled and ammunitioned, it is invincible, except fraud or famine do assault, or conspire against it.

The damaged and destroyed castles were left to decay even further and the ruins allowed to become overgrown. In the course of time these ruins were picked over by the local populace, who again removed cartloads of masonry to be used on other building projects, including barns and houses. One of the more fortunate beneficiaries was the Middleton family, who were of Parliamentary sympathies, and had managed to capture intact their own family home of Chirk castle in 1646, which was being held by Royalist troops. In 1659 Middleton was restored to his lands and, with Oliver Cromwell dead, was openly supporting a restoration of the monarchy. However, he was premature in his assumption that Charles Stuart, the son of the executed King Charles, should be returned to the throne. Chirk castle was attacked by a force led by General Lambert and subjected to an artillery bombardment, which caused substantial damage. In 1660 the monarchy was restored and Middleton was vindicated in his support in favour of the restoration of the royal family. In return for his support Middleton was rewarded by being granted £30,000 for the repair of Chirk castle.

The length of time for which a castle of the medieval period could withstand a siege during the English Civil War depended on a number of factors, the most important of which was its state of preparedness. The garrisons in most, if not all, of those castles held in Wales for the king knew it was only a question of time before they were invested. Both sides were fully aware that gunpowder artillery was a major factor in bringing about an end to a siege. Some castles surrendered after only a few days, others held out for weeks and months. In the most extreme cases a very few managed to withstand the siege tactics for years.

84   Carew castle was fought over and changed hands a number of times during the Civil War.
Parliamentary forces captured the castle in 1645 and it was slighted to prevent its use by Royalist
forces

Parliamentarian officers knew it was in their best interests to end a siege as
quickly as possible. As in previous operations of this type, they realised that any
prolonged siege would severely strain the resources of their supply column and
morale could be deeply affected. The defenders, for their part, realised that in
most cases relief forces or reinforcements were highly unlikely, but they knew
the longer they held the castle the more enemy troops they diverted from the
field of battle.

All castles in Wales, large and small, were considered important to either
side in the war, for they knew these fortifications could be used as centres of
operations. For example, the relatively small castle of Carew saw much fighting
and changing of hands, before the Parliamentarian forces finally captured it for
good in 1645 *(84)*. They slighted the defences, causing much damage to the
south wall in particular and a tower was demolished. The story was a similar
one wherever Parliamentarian forces captured a castle. They considered the
slighting of a castle to be a fact of war and essential in denying it to Royalist
forces at any time in the future. It also meant that with the destruction of a
castle's defences, it did not have to be garrisoned by Parliamentarian forces.
There was one exception to this rule, though, at Chepstow castle which had
been held for the king. The castle was besieged twice during the war, and
when it fell to the Parliamentarian forces on the second occasion they actually
installed a garrison. Instead of slighting the castle the garrison set about

reinforcing the fabric of the walls by piling up earth against the southern curtain wall and the bases of the towers. This move was designed to absorb the force of impact by cannonballs. It was cheap, simple and yet highly effective against the solid iron projectiles of seventeenth–century artillery.

Whilst one can see a certain rationale to this line of reasoning, it did have a negative side. Slighting of such defences also meant denial to one's own side and troops could not always be billeted together in large centralised groups as the grounds of a castle would have allowed. From these sites the garrisons could have extended their influence over the surrounding area. But armies of the seventeenth century did not want to occupy territory with permanent garrisons. They were more inclined to move on to subdue the next military target, and should it be a castle, they would remove it in the form of slighting. It was the agrarian way of life in Wales that meant once the centre of resistance around a castle had been defeated the organised fighting virtually came to an end. Although Wales had almost unanimously sided with the king, after a military engagement there was no real need for an army of occupation. Peace invariably returned and life went back to a semblance of normality with farming and trading continuing.

The fighting in Wales saw the shifting of allegiances as the war moved across the country. The Royalists and Parliamentarians had fought one another a number of times since the battle of Edgehill on 24 October 1642, but it was not until 1644 that the war proper came to Wales. One such battle of quickly shifting sides occurred at Laugharne, a small town with a castle commanding the approaches to the River Taf as it flows into the estuary in Carmarthen Bay.

In 1644 Laugharne was held for parliament, one of a small but growing number of areas beginning to take sides against the king *(85)*. The Royalists dispatched Sir Charles Gerard to the area and ordered him to capture the castle. He arrived in early June 1644, and so sudden and successful was his campaign that by the end of the month he had also taken the castles at Kidwelly, Carmarthen, Newcastle Emlyn and Cardigan, covering an area of more than 30 miles in radius. To the west of Gerard's centre of operations lay Haverfordwest castle, which was being successfully blockaded by a Royalist fleet. The Parliamentary garrison, under the command of Major-General Rowland Laugharne, was cut off and forced to retire southwards into the safe strongholds of Tenby and Pembroke.

It proved to be only a temporary victory for the Royalists, because three weeks after the king's army had been defeated at the battle of Marston Moor on 2 July 1644, Gerard removed the bulk of his forces and marched back into England. Behind him he left a rearguard force and garrisons to hold the castles he had recently seized. One of these was Laugharne castle, under the command of Lieutenant-Colonel Sir William Russell. Gerard must have realised that he was being observed and known his movements were inviting the Parliamentarians to attack his weakened garrisons.

85 Laugharne castle suffered a fierce and intense battle, including artillery bombardment. The castle fell to Parliamentarian troops in the early hours of the morning of 3 November 1644

In October, Major-General Laugharne deemed it the right time to move against the garrison at Laugharne, which had been reduced in size. Incidentally, there was no family connection between the Major-General and the town and castle of the same name. The castle was invested on the evening of 28 October 1644, with Laugharne's troops taking up their positions on the heights about 2 miles to the north of the castle, from where they could descend directly onto their target. Major-General Laugharne's forces had been reinforced and his artillery train included a powerful weapon known as a demi-culverin, which had been landed from a ship. The siege had started and a bombardment aimed at reducing the garrison immediately commenced. The garrison within the castle were holding onto their position, but they were suffering casualties as the cannonballs struck home.

The artillery bombardment continued from a site only about 1 mile to the east of the castle, but after three days, the gunners realised they were not making much impression on the target. The engagement looked as though it were in danger of becoming a protracted affair. Laugharne then ordered his artillery to move to a site known as Fern Hill, to the west of the castle. From here, his gunners could fire at the gatehouse. He also ordered 200 musketeers from his force to move into the town and capture it. The castle and the garrison were now completely cut off, but they still held on determinedly to their positions. On the evening of 30 October the Parliamentarians seized the town gate and were able to move their artillery into a position in the town from where it could fire directly down the main street and at the castle gatehouse. The bombardment continued over the next two days, until finally on 2 November, Laugharne's troops rushed forward to capture the outer gate of the castle at around 11pm.

The fighting continued until about 1am on the morning of 3 November, when the defenders called for a ceasefire in order to permit terms of surrender to be discussed. Having agreed on acceptable terms the defenders of Laugharne castle surrendered at 7am. The garrison of some 200 men marched out and their officers left to join the Royalist garrison at Carmarthen. The action had cost the Parliamentarians only ten killed and about thirty wounded. The defenders had lost thirty-three killed and a large number of wounded. The castle at Laugharne was described by one Parliamentarian as: 'One of the holds from whence our forces and the country received the greatest annoyance.' The castle remains were slighted and sections of the walls were demolished to render it useless to the Royalists. The action was but a relatively minor skirmish in the overall scheme of the war, but had it been left in Royalist hands, it would have continued to allow raiding parties to attack deep into Parliamentary territory.

Lying on the eastern boundaries of Wales is Raglan castle, which during the Civil War was a very powerful site, well defended and with a reliable garrison. The defences were solid and strong, including artillery *(86)*. It was held for the king by the incredibly wealthy Henry Somerset, who had been created a marquis in 1643. As an indication of his wealth, it is said the marquis supported the garrison of the castle with a sum of around £40,000. A written account by the Royalist supporter Richard Symonds tells how the estate of the marquis was 'esteemed 24 Thowsand Pounds per annum'. He relates how in 1645 the garrison of Raglan castle was around 300 men, all being: 'constantly paid'. Furthermore, the marquis is believed to have donated some £1,000,000 to the king's war chest.

Apart from the strength of the castle's walls, the garrison set about to construct forward defensive earthworks and fill large wicker baskets, known as gabions, for the protection of gunners and musketeers. These outer works complemented the water-filled moat which surrounded the great hall or keep, and made the site a formidable target to attack. The defenders could be formed in depth both inside and beyond the boundaries from where their artillery could fire back at the attackers. The order to invest the castle was given to Colonel Thomas Morgan, who complied in June 1646. He was an experienced soldier and commanded his forces well. Even so, he found he could not advance against the castle as the campaign entered July.

Within his force Morgan had a captain of engineers, John Hooper, who had constructed a battery from where the Parliamentary artillery was able to destroy several cannon on the castle walls. Hooper set about instructing his men to dig trenches, known as 'saps', which would allow their artillery to be

86 Raglan castle, the site of a fierce battle with artillery and engineering actions. It finally surrendered in August 1646 and was ordered to be slighted. However, the destruction never happened because it was too difficult to demolish the site

moved closer to the castle while sheltered from the defenders' musket fire. In early August, Sir Thomas Fairfax, commander-in-chief, arrived at the siege to take stock of the situation. More artillery was being brought on to the site, including a huge mortar nicknamed 'Roaring Meg', which had been trans-ported to the siege by Colonel John Birch, governor of Hereford. By now Hooper's trenches were only 60 yards from the walls of the castle. The standard weapons in the siege train of the Parliamentarians artillery force, such as culverins, would have had a telling impact at such close quarters, but the mortars would have been most useful that close to the walls of the castle.

Mortars at the time fired hollow spheres, known as shells, which were filled with gunpowder and fitted with a rudimentary fuse to detonate them with an explosive force. The barrels of mortars were set to fire their projectiles at very high angles of trajectory in order to shoot them over the walls in a lobbing action. They were short-range weapons, hence the reason for the trenches being located so close to the walls of Raglan castle. In firing the mortar, timing was essential, particularly when lighting the fuse of the shell just prior to use. An experienced gunner serving a mortar could calculate with some degree of precision the optimum moment when he had to light the fuse and exactly what its length should be for burning.

Mortar shells, being filled with gunpowder, were designed to explode, causing a great deal of damage to the surrounding target area, killing and wounding troops. A normal, solid-iron cannonball, on the other hand, caused

87 The main tower and water defences of Raglan castle, which made it such a formidable target. The fighting was fierce and the garrison was allowed to surrender with full military honours

only localised damage when it smashed walls, which could be repaired. The blast from a mortar shell when it exploded could also cause fires. Therefore, in the face of such a formidable artillery train, the marquis realised he had no other option but to surrender. His resolve was reaffirmed on 14 August, when new trenches were identified as they approached the walls of the castles.

It was agreed that a formal surrender should take place on 19 August *(87)*. On the agreed day and at the appointed time, the marquis awaited the arrival of the Parliamentary delegation in the great hall of the castle, the walls of which had been so badly battered by artillery that he 'could see through the window the General [Fairfax] with all his officers entering the Outward Court, as if a floodgate had been left open.'

When the Parliamentarian forces entered Raglan castle they found much in the way of munitions and twenty pieces of artillery of varying size, but only one barrel of gunpowder. Given the lack of this essential supply for musketeers and artillery, the Parliamentary forces were puzzled as to how the defenders had been able to keep firing their weapons for such a long time. As they searched the castle further they discovered the answer. With great ingenuity the garrison had built a gunpowder mill with which it had been possible to make at least one barrel of gunpowder per day. Given their limited resources this was truly remarkable. The preparations made by the garrison prior to the siege had been so complete that they had been able to cast their own cannonballs and musket balls.

The chaplain to Sir Thomas Fairfax, Joshua Sprigge, wrote later of the action in a book called *Anglia Rediviva*, in which he states how the obstinacy of the garrison at 'Raglan and Pendennis, like winter fruit, hung long on'. The garrison was allowed to march out from the castle 'with their Horses and Armes, with Colours flying, Drums beating, Trumpets sounding.' Behind them the garrison left their sick and wounded along with those outside the terms of pardon as laid down in the treaty of surrender. One of these was the marquis, who later died as a prisoner in London. After the fall of the castle and the removal of useful items and objects of value, Raglan was slighted for the usual reasons. One account of the slighting, written in *c.*1670, tells how:

Afterwards it [the castle] was demolished, the lead & timber carried to Monmouth there by water to rebuild Bristoll bridg after the last fire, & the woods in ye 3 parkes destroyed. The tower Mellin was undermined and supported with timber till 2 sid[e]s of 6 were cut through; the timber being burnt it fel downe in a lump and soe rema[i]ns. After ye surrender the country people were summoned as to a Randevow with spads and pixaxes to draw ye mote in hope of treasure; that failing they were sett to cut the stanks [banks or dams] of the great fishpond, where was a great store of carpe & other fish. The artificiall roofe of the hall could not safely be taken downe, remained above 20 yeares till it perish by ye weather. There remains about 30 valts of cellers, bridgs and other roomes at present. The large valt of the tower bridg & most curious arches of the chappell with many valts [are] totally destroyed.

The method of approach employed at the siege of Raglan castle to advance the artillery was actually standard practice. It had originated in Europe and its methods had proved so successful that its use soon spread. It was a relatively straightforward tactic, if somewhat labour intensive. First a parallel trench was dug some 600–700 yards out from the fortification under siege, and very often completely encircled the site being attacked. From this trench, which was just out of effective reach of the defenders' artillery fire, a number of points would be selected from where an assault or several assaults could be made. The engineers then dug a series of 'saps' leading towards the target. They used a 'zig-zag' method of approach in order to prevent the defenders from firing down the length of the trench, which could have caused casualties. As the men dug they threw the spoil from the workings up to form earthworks to add height to the parapets for the added protection of the troops. The distance advanced was usually dictated by the maximum effective range of defenders' artillery and that of the attackers' artillery. This was usually set at about 300 yards. Under good directions engineers might press a sap forward at the rate of about 146 yards in twenty-four hours. At that point a second parallel of trench works would be dug, with additional earthworks being thrown up in front of it to serve as protection for siege-artillery emplacements, which were brought forward by the gunners. Under cover of fire from these guns the labouring engineers would continue the approach and dig further 'saps' towards the target. All the time the siege guns would be firing against the ramparts in an effort to force the defenders to take cover from the attackers' artillery. This was designed to reduce the effects of the defenders' artillery.

If a breach was made in the wall at this point the attackers could assault and storm the positions. However, there was always the possibility that the defenders might rally and counter-attack, forcing the attackers to withdraw. This happened at Pembroke castle when Cromwell's men rushed to the breach in the town walls. Should the defenders continue to resist then a third parallel would have to be dug and more artillery would be brought up to fire at the defenders. The type of artillery pieces at this stage could also include mortars, which would be used to lob bombs at high angles inside the defences. More often than not it took no more than two days' bombardment from this third parallel to sufficiently silence the defenders' resolve. The marquis at Raglan would have been aware of this, and obviously in a move to save the lives of his men he elected to surrender the castle.

It was not just those castles held by Royalists that were besieged. There were instances when the situation was reversed and those castles held in Wales for parliament were attacked by Royalist forces. When each side raised their standards for war in 1642, Pembroke declared for parliament and the castle was garrisoned by forces commanded by John Poyer, the town mayor. Throughout the winter of 1642–1643 the garrison strengthened their defences and laid in extra provisions for the siege they knew must come. Part of these preparations included the landing of supplies brought to the castle by ships, which had sailed into the estuary and navigated their way up the river.

The castle was not completely invested by Royalist forces and far from being totally isolated. This allowed it to be used a base of operations from where Colonel Rowland Laugharne could campaign, one of his actions being the successful attacking and seizing of Laugharne castle in 1644. The garrison were in a very strong position and were able to hold out without suffering any undue privations. With strong defences and the capability of being revictualled by sea, there was not much for the garrison to fear. As long as the Royalists did not bring mortars against them or succeed in blockading the river they were safe. However, before they could be put to the test the war ended and their situation was relieved. In 1645 King Charles was captured after being defeated and arrested. The Civil War was declared at an end. Some of the garrison within the castle did march away, one of whom was Colonel Rowland Laugharne.

However, it was not a simple act to disband such a powerful garrison as that which served the defences at Pembroke castle *(88)*. There were many Parliamentarians who were aggrieved over lack of payment and promises, which had been reneged on by army councils. One of those greatly annoyed at this poor state of affairs was John Poyer, who had commanded the garrison at the castle during the war. He demanded due recompense for services rendered by himself and his men. When this restitution was not forthcoming he stayed firmly in charge of the immensely strong castle and the walled town. This state of affairs lasted until 1648, when Poyer for some inexplicable and unexpected reason declared for the king. This was betrayal of the highest order and something which parliament could not ignore.

Oliver Cromwell as Lieutenant-General of the Parliamentary army ordered in Colonel Fleming to act as constable of Pembroke. He was attacked and driven off by Colonel Powell, who had remained with John Poyer and the remainder of the garrison. The spirited attack had not only driven Fleming out of the town, it had also succeeded in capturing two pieces of artillery. Not one to give up his duty, Fleming returned to attack in April. During the ensuing battle he was killed by troops under the command of Colonel Powell.

Returning to the scene came Rowland Laugharne, who had been under arrest in London on suspicion of being involved in a Royalist plot. This suspicion turned to conclusive evidence when he joined forces with Colonel Powell and between them raised a force of some 8,000 men with Royalist sympathies. They moved on St Fagans and on 8 May 1648 appeared to be on the verge of gaining a victory against local Parliamentary forces, when a force of dragoons, commanded by Colonel John Okey, and others of the New Model Army, attacked, driving them back.

88 Pembroke castle was such a nuisance to Parliamentarian troops that Oliver Cromwell was ordered to take charge of operations personally. He brought a strong artillery force to bear on the castle

89 After seven weeks Pembroke castle succumbed to the attackers and in March 1647 the last major stronghold surrendered to Parliamentarian forces

90 Tenby was a fortified site and walled town, which was fought over extensively during the Civil War, finally surrendering in 1647

Incensed by this treachery, Oliver Cromwell travelled to Pembroke to take personal command of operations. He arrived on 24 May leading a force of some 6,000 men and immediately set about the investment of the town and castle. His artillery train was well equipped, and included several naval cannon brought ashore specially for the operation. Cromwell contrived to make his preparations for the remainder of May, during which time there were minor skirmishes between the two sides. Cromwell had also to deal with Tenby in the same month, for the Parliamentarian garrison had changed sides to support the Royalist cause when their commander, Colonel Rice Powell, was absent. It did not take long to reduce the town walls with his artillery train. The garrison were dealt with and he captured twenty further cannon which were put to use at other sieges as the warring was coming to an end in Wales. Meanwhile at Pembroke, the river approach to the castle was blockaded and the town and castle were completely surrounded on all sides by batteries of artillery and infantry. The besiegers succeeded in setting fire to a number of buildings and managed to blast a breach in the town walls. Despite this, the defenders held out and engaged Cromwell's men in fierce street fighting as they attempted to enter the town through the breach in the walls between 15 and 16 June. All the while the besiegers were growing stronger as more and more reinforcements continued to arrive and bolster Cromwell's forces.

On 1 July the heavy siege guns of Cromwell's artillery opened their bombardment. The outcome was still far from being clear cut and the defenders appeared ever more determined to hold out against Cromwell's forces. In the end, however, the traitors were themselves betrayed, when someone divulged the source the drinking water used by the defenders. It was immediately cut off. Isolated from any would-be Royalist reinforcements and with no water the defenders of Pembroke were growing weaker by the day. Left with no option the three commanding figures, Poyer, Powell and Laugharne sued for peace and terms of surrender *(89)*.

The garrison was allowed to disperse, but the three leaders were arrested and taken to London, where they were condemned to death by parliament. In an unusual move the three convicted ringleaders were allowed to draw 'lots' as to who would be executed and who would have their sentences commuted. They drew lots and John Poyer lost. He forfeited his life for his actions before a firing squad in Covent Garden.

It had taken Cromwell seven weeks to subdue Pembroke. The slighting of the castle and town walls was inevitable and Cromwell ordered: 'demolish [Pembroke] castle, so as that [it] may not be possest by the enemy.' In keeping with with this order, troops placed charges of gunpowder in the towers of the castle and blasted out sections of the walls.

Pembroke castle may have been a problem for the Parliamentarians with such doggedness of a garrison, which at times was undecided as to whose side to support in the Civil War. However, for pure determination the defence of Harlech castle cannot be bettered. Like the other large castles, it was held for the king by a garrison, in this case commanded by Colonel William Owen of Brogyntyn, who had taken up occupation of the site in early 1644. The investing Parliamentarian force was commanded by Colonel Mytton, who was hard pressed to bring about its surrender. Before the war the castle was known to be in a poor state of repairs and there appears to be no record of the castle ever being repaired or fortified to withstand a siege involving artillery. On the morning of 16 March 1647, the last remaining troops of the garrison, comprising fourteen gentlemen and twenty-eight soldiers, marched out of Harlech castle. It was the last major Royalist stronghold on the mainland to surrender, having been under constant siege since late June 1646.

Other Welsh castles across the length and breadth of the country would find themselves the centrepiece of battles or sieges during the hard-fought Civil War *(90)*. Picton castle, lying to the south-east of Haverfordwest, was attacked and blown up by Parliamentarian forces in 1648. In 1643 the castle had been held for the king by Sir Richard Philips with a garrison of Royalist troops. In 1645 it was attacked again and stormed by Parliamentary forces, who captured it by employing means that were less than honourable. According to the account, an incident occurred during the siege when a Parliamentary trooper, under a flag of truce, rode up to a window to deliver a message to the garrison commander. Receiving the message was a nursemaid holding Sir Richard's infant son, Erasmus Phillips, and on her leaning out of the window too far, the trooper snatched the baby from her arms. The Parliamentarian commander ordered the garrison to surrender in exchange for the life of the baby. Sir Richard evacuated the castle, but the Parliamentarian commander felt so ashamed at the actions of his troops that he did not order the immediate destruction of the castle. That would be completed later during another action.

Other castles to be involved in the fighting included Aberystwyth, which was attacked by Parliamentarian forces in 1646, when it was held by Colonel Roger Whitley for the king. This was not the first time the castle had been attacked. In 1644, the Royalist garrison had mounted a counter-attack against the Parliamentarian besiegers attacking nearby Llanbarden. However, their mission failed and thirteen of them were drowned in the millpond as they retreated back to the safety of the castle. Brecon castle served for a short time as a refuge for King Charles after his defeat at the battle of Naseby on 14 June 1645. The castle was later dismantled by the local populace to prevent it from being used as a fortified site by either side. Other castles, such as Chirk, Chepstow, Denbigh and Howarden, all served their part in the fighting. In fact, Denbigh even served as a refuge for Charles I following his defeat at Rowton Heath near Chester on 24 September 1645. He remained there for three days, secure behind the stout defences of the castle's walls and the gatehouse with its three octagonal towers, which added to the strength of the castle. Between April and October 1646 Denbigh castle was besieged by Parliamentarian forces, who dug extensive earthworks around the castle, where their artillery was sited to batter the walls. The castle was held by Colonel Salisbury with a garrison of 500 men. As the siege dragged on it became clear that a relief force was not forthcoming and the defenders sued for favourable terms of surrender. Upon relinquishing the site, the Parliamentarians used Denbigh castle as a prison and manned it with a reduced garrison.

Perhaps one of the saddest fates of all Welsh castles was that which befell Caerphilly castle in either 1646 or 1647. The great castle was not directly involved in the fighting and was never subjected to a siege during the whole of the Civil War. The reason for this has been put down to the water obstacles outside the castle walls. It is true, these defences are formidable, but with the right equipment a besieging force would have eventually overcome these features. Admittedly, it would have taken time and been costly in lives but they could have been assailed. It may have been realised that the cost of attacking the castle would have been too great in casualty rate and this probably prevented either side from attacking Caerphilly castle. Despite this, the castle was subjected to severe slighting. Some sources say this was committed by Royalist forces in 1646. Other sources say it was damaged by Parliamentarian forces in 1647 *(91)*. Whichever side completed the task, the slighting was localised but it proved a point and the castle did not play a direct part in the fighting.

91 Caerphilly Castle, where the slighting is blamed on both Royalist and Parliamentarian forces in 1647. The tower, seen here, is evidence of that destruction along with other lesser signs

The walls of the medieval castles, which had been occupied as centres of operations during the Civil War, had been thickened 200 years earlier, when gunpowder artillery made its first significant appearance on the battlefield. At the time when the walls were thickened, the move had been effective against the slow-firing cannon, which shot their stone projectiles at a relatively low velocity. However, in the intervening years artillery had evolved into cannon with barrels of cast iron, which used more powerful gunpowder that had been refined to produce higher velocities. The projectiles were now much heavier, being made from cast iron and the cannon themselves were more accurate and their rate of fire had been increased. Against such weapons the walls of such old castles, even with improved defences, stood no chance of survival. The walls crumbled in the face of such concentrated bombardments, and even with the best efforts of the defenders to repair the damage, the result was inevitable. The time taken to reduce a castle did vary with its size and state of preparedness, but the mere presence of artillery very nearly always brought about the garrison's surrender.

No one had thought to maintain the strength of the castles, because they were believed to be obsolete. For this very reason they had not been upgraded to keep pace with military developments. Again, no one had thought that such old defences would ever be thrust into the frontline of war, and certainly not a conflict where such powerful weapons as artillery would be used. The garrisons holding the castles were often far too large for the accommodation available. As a result the conditions soon became very uncomfortable and deteriorated to a point where health was threatened. Larger castles such as Pembroke and Raglan were better equipped to take a large garrison, but the smaller castles, such as Carew and Laugharne, could not have been very pleasant places in which to reside during a siege. The fact that these castles had been used at all was a testimony to their enduring image as strongholds. They had stood up to their new-found role, but in the end it was the weight of firepower levelled against them and the improved siege tactics which brought about their demise.

In Wales the general consensus had been to support the king and his army. There had been no large-scale, set-piece battles as there had been at sites in England, such as Naseby, Marston Moor or Newbury. Instead the brunt of the fighting had been borne by the castles of Wales. They had played no small part in the war and even shown how, despite their age, if they were in a state of good repair and with a strong garrison, they could feature in seventeenth-century warfare. The First Civil War could be said to have ended on 30 January 1649, when King Charles was executed in Whitehall, London. Two of the fifty-nine men who signed his death warrant were Welshmen: John Jones, member for Meirionnydd, and Thomas Wogan, member for Cardigan. On 4 January that year parliament had established the Commonwealth, an act that was grimly and angrily received across Wales. Under the new order Wales was seen as being no more than the 'dark corners of the land'. When Oliver Cromwell died in September 1658, his son Richard had been viewed as the natural successor. However, he proved too weak for the task and resigned in May 1659, thereby leaving the way open for the king. Wales had not waited for the official moment to arrive and in August 1659 at Wrexham, Thomas Myddleton proclaimed that the late king's son, Charles, be recognised as king. It would not be until 1660, with the Restoration of the monarchy and King Charles II, that Wales could finally rest at ease from fear of further war.

WORLD WARS AND WELSH CASTLES

Almost 300 years later one would have thought that Welsh castles had no role to play in modern twentieth-century warfare. However, despite this assumption, some sites proved to have some degree of service left in them and played a small, yet significant part during the Second World War. The site of St Donats, for example, which had a rich history, was taken over by the British army, who remained in occupancy until 1962. Similarly, Dolbarden was taken over by the Ministry of Works in 1941 and used for various purposes. Another prominent

92   The curtain wall and towers surrounding White Castle, below which is the wet or flooded moat

site to be pressed into service during the Second World War was Cardigan castle, which had a small concrete pillbox built on the walls among the crenellations, from where a machine gun could be fired. It was not a major emplacement in the proper sense of the word, being more suited to observation roles for the local Home Guard units. Nevertheless, it shows how medieval castles could and were often pressed to serve a purpose in twentieth-century warfare.

On 10 May 1941 England received a most unexpected visitor in the form of Rudolf Hess, the deputy party leadership of the Nazi Party. In an attempt to broker a unilateral negotiated peace between England and Germany, Hess piloted an aircraft in an unauthorised flight and crash-landed in Scotland. He was immediately arrested and interned for the duration of the war, part of which was spent in a mental institution in Abergavenny. On occasions he was escorted to the grounds of White Castle (also known as Llantilio castle) in Monmouthshire, close to Raglan castle. The castle had been acquired by the Ministry of Works in 1941 *(92)*. Here he was allowed to take exercise under strict supervision. This is surely one of the most unusual roles for any medieval castle.

England had been conquered as the result of one decisive battle on Senlac Hill in October 1066. For over 400 years the Normans and their succeeding descendants and ruling dynasties would seek to dominate Wales and control the Welsh. Large areas of the country were to fall under English rule, but the Welsh always seemed able to fight back. It cost many lives on both sides and the English had to mount successive campaigns. But, somehow complete total rule over the country avoided them. Indeed, it could be argued that the Welsh had the last say in the matter when Henry Tudor ascended the throne of England in 1485 to rule as Henry VII. A ruling dynasty of Tudor monarchs had been established, with Welsh ancestry, and would control England for 118 years.

Welsh castles, both great and small, remain in all their splendour and continue to awe visitors, inspire artists and attract historians from all over the world, who come to study them. Today a number of sites serve as backdrops to public displays for historical presentations and special events, which re-enact periods of their long and prestigious histories. These displays range from the medieval period, depicting Owain Glyn Dwr, through to the Civil War, with artillery firings and, organised by such offices as Cadw, they are designed to give an added sense of realism. These colourful spectacles help engender a greater sense of history to the visitors as they wander around the grounds of the castle. In summing up the magnificence of these Welsh castles, which have withstood so much war and destruction, one cannot help but think of what Sir Richard Colt Hoare wrote of Raglan castle in his journal, later published as *Journeys*, for 7 June 1802: 'I cannot but regret whenever I view this grand relict of baronial magnificence that it has been for so long neglected and uninhabited'. To single out just one remark to cover all castles in Wales is a difficult choice, but those words of Sir Richard sum up everything very succinctly. Today the magnificent castles in Wales are preserved for the public to view and enjoy and they continue to symbolise the rich history of Wales.

TIMELINE

1039	Gruffydd ap Llywellan defeats the Mercians at Crossford.
1066	The battle of Hastings, the Norman Conquest and William the Conqueror proclaimed king.
1081	William travels to St Davids.
1081	Robert of Rhuddlan captures Gruffydd ap Cynan of Gwynedd.
1087	Death of King William the Conqueror; William Rufus proclaimed king and rules as William II.
1090	Philip de Braose seizes Radnor and establishes himself at Builth; Bernard de Newmarch (de Neufmarche) takes over Brycheiniog and establishes castle at Brecon.
1093	Death of Rhys ap Tewdwr.
1100	Death of William II; Henry proclaimed king and reigns as Henry I.
1109	Ceredigion granted to Gilbert de Clare who conquers region by 1111.
1114	Henry I invades Wales.
1121	Henry I invades Wales.
1135	Death of Henry I; Stephen proclaimed king.
1154	Death of King Stephen; Henry II proclaimed king.
1157	Owen of north Wales performs homage to King Henry; Henry II attacks Anglesey.
1158	Rhys ap Gruffydd ruler of south Wales.
1170	Death of Owain the Great; battle of Pentraeth.
1189	Death of King Henry II; Richard I (The Lionheart) proclaimed king.
1194	Battle of Porthaethwy; battle of Coedanau.
1197	Death of Rhys, son of Gruffydd.
1199	Death of Richard I; John proclaimed king.
1200	William Marshall, earl of Pembroke takes office.
1216	Death of King John; William Marshall, earl of Pembroke, regent to Henry, aged nine years old; Henry III proclaimed king.

1240	Death of Llywelyn ap Iowerth, 'The Great', Prince of north Wales.
1272	Death of Henry III; Edward I proclaimed king; Llywelyn ap Gruffydd, grandson of Llywelyn the Great, refused homage to Edward.
1274	Edward arrives in England to take the throne.
1277	Edward's first Welsh campaign; Llywelyn surrenders.
1282	Edward's second Welsh campaign. Llywelyn killed.
1284	Statute of Rhuddlan.
1294	Revolt of Madog of Wales.
1307	Death of Edward I; Edward II proclaimed king.
1327	Death of Edward II; Edward III proclaimed king.
1377	Death of Edward III; Richard II proclaimed king.
1399	Death of Richard II; Henry IV proclaimed king.
1400	Owain Glyn Dwr begins campaign against English.
1401	Welsh rebellion spreads.
1404	Glyn Dwr captures Harlech castle and holds parliament at Machynlleth.
1405	Henry Prince of Wales captures Coity castle.
1406	Prince Henry defeats the Welsh.
1408	Capture of Aberystwyth.
1409	Surrender of Harlech to English.
1413	Death of Henry IV; Henry V proclaimed king.
1415	English victory at battle of Agincourt, 21 October; date believed for death of Owain Glyn Dwr.
1422	Death of Henry V; Henry VI proclaimed king.
1461	Death of Henry VI.
1483	Richard III proclaimed king.
1485	Death of Richard III; Henry VII proclaimed king.
1501	Arthur Prince of Wales marries Catharine of Aragon.
1502	Arthur Prince of Wales dies.
1504	Prince Henry proclaimed Prince of Wales.
1509	Death of Henry VII; Henry VIII proclaimed king.
1536	Act of Union between England and Wales.
1547	Death of Henry VIII; Edward VI proclaimed king.
1553	Death of Edward VI; Mary Tudor proclaimed queen.
1558	Death of Mary Tudor; Elizabeth Tudor proclaimed queen.
1603	Death of Elizabeth Tudor.
1642–1651	The English Civil War; fighting in Wales.

GAZETTEER TO WELSH CASTLES

Beaumaris (SH 328707): Sited on the island of Anglesey, 8km (5 miles) north-east of the Menai bridge. Built *c.*1295–1300, but unfinished. Concentric shape with square inner bailey and 'D-plan' wall towers. Cadw.

Bronllys (SO 149348): Powys, 13km (8miles) north-east of Brecon. Round keep and motte and bailey, started in 1176. Cadw.

Caernarvon (SH 477626): Gwynedd. Started in 1283 with building continuing until 1330. Curtain walls with firing galleries and towers. Extremely strong defences. Cadw.

Caerphilly (ST 155871): Glamorgan. Building started in 1271 and much of the original defences remain surrounded by artificial lakes to form water defences. Cadw.

Cardiff (ST 180767): Glamorgan. Motte and bailey on site of Roman fort. Shell keep from twelfth century, but greatly altered in nineteenth century. Telephone: 02920 222253. Website: www.qdg.org.uk

Carew (SN 045037): Dyfed, 6.4km (4 miles) north-east of Pembroke (*qv*). Parts dating from 1200 and building continuing through thirteenth century. Greatly altered in sixteenth century. Telephone: 01646 651782. Website: www.pembrokeshirecoast.org.uk

Carreg Cennen (SN 668190): Dyfed, 4.8km (3 miles) south-east Llandeilo. Curtain walls with towers and rectangular outer bailey. Fabric dates from thirteenth and fourteenth centuries. Cadw.

Chepstow (ST 533941): Gwent. Remains of curtain walls dating from eleventh century with additions dating from twelfth and thirteenth centuries. Cadw.

Chirk (SJ 281377): Clwyd, 11km (7 miles) north-west of Oswestry. Built between 1289 and 1295. Large round towers at corner stations with curtain walls. Altered and rebuilt in seventeenth century.

Cilgerran (SN 195431): Dyfed, 3.2km (2 miles) south-east of Cardigan. Large wall towers and gatehouse with domestic quarters. Cadw.

Coity (SS 923816): Glamorgan, 3.2km (2 miles) north of Bridgend. Curtain walls, gatehouse and square keep dating from twelfth century. Additional building in thirteenth and fourteenth centuries. Cadw.

Conwy (SH 784774): Gwynedd. Built between 1283 and 1287 with 'D-plan' towers. Outer bailey, round wall towers and curtain walls. Cadw.

Criccieth (SH 500377): Gwynedd. Built between 1285 and 1292 with unusual polygonal curtain walls lacking towers. Cadw.

Degannwy (SH 781794): Gwynedd, 3.2km (2 miles) north of Conwy. Built between 1244 and 1254 on site of ninth-century fortification. Used during the campaign of 1277.

Denbigh (SJ 059660): Clwyd. Built in 1282 and completed in 1285. Octagonal walls enclosing polygonal keep. Additional fortifications added in 1295. Cadw.

Dolbarden (SH 586598): Gwynedd, 12.8 km (8 miles) south of Bangor. Curtain walls and towers dating from thirteenth century. Cadw.

Dolwyddelan (SH 722523): Gwynedd, 9.6km (6 miles) south-west of Betws-y-Coed. Small keep of two storeys, dating from thirteenth century and additional features from fifteenth century. Cadw.

Dynevor (SN 611217): Dyfed, 1.6km (1 mile) west of Llandeilo. Curtain wall dating from twelfth century, but parts rebuilt in fifteenth century. Round keep dating from thirteenth century. Cadw.

Ewloe (SJ 288675): Clwyd, 19.3km (12 miles) west of Chester. Curtain walls with 'D-plan' towers dating from thirteenth century along with round corner tower. Cadw.

Flint (SJ 247733): Clwyd. Built between 1277 and 1286 with square inner bailey with curtain walls and three round corner towers. Moated, but now dry. Cadw.

Grosmont (SO 405244): Gwent, 22.5km (14 miles) south-west of Hereford. Started in twelfth century and work continuing until fourteenth century, with gatehouse and wall towers being added in thirteenth century. Cadw.

Harlech (SH 581313): Gwynedd. Built between 1283 and 1289. Low curtain walls with towers and gatehouse. Cadw.

Haverfordwest (SM 953157): Dyfed. Polygonal bailey dating from fourteenth century. Remains much altered but curtain walls and square wall tower evident.

Hawarden (SJ 319653): Clwyd, 11.2km (7 miles) west of Chester. Dating from the early thirteenth century. Srong barbican and polygonal bailey with round keep.

Hen Domen (SO 214980): Powys, 3.2km (2 miles) north-west of Montgomery. Motte and bailey with double rampart and ditch.

Kidwelly (N 409071): Dyfed, 12.8km (8 miles) north-west of Llanelli. Impressive gatehouse and conglomeration of walls and buildings, dating from mid-thirteenth century. Curtain walls and keep. Hall and chapel added between 1280 and 1300, with work continuing until fourteenth century. Cadw.

Laugharne (SN 302107): Dyfed. Walls and bailey dating from thirteenth century with additional work being completed in sixteenth century. Inner bailey of four storeys, but outer bailey lost. Cadw.

Llanstephan (SN 351101): Dyfed, 12.8km (8 miles) south-west of Carmarthen. Curtain walls and bailey from twelfth century. Evidence of architectural changes evident in gatehouse, which was altered in thirteenth century and again in fifteenth century. Cadw.

Manorbier (SS 064978): Dyfed, 9.6km (6 miles) south-west of Tenby. Polygonal curtain wall dating from 1230. Castle built in twelfth century with additional work being carried out in thirteenth century. Private ownership but open to public. Telephone: 01834 871394.

Monmouth (SO 507129): Gwent. Dating from eleventh century and work continuing through thirteenth and fourteenth centuries. Round tower slighted in 1647 during English Civil War. Cadw.

Montgomery (SO 2219667): Powys. Built in 1224 with gatehouse and oval inner bailey. Now in ruins. Cadw.

Ogmore (SS 882769): Glamorgan, 4.8km (3 miles) south-west of Bridgend. Progressively added to through three centuries, twelfth century to fourteenth century. Rectangular keep and curtain walls. Cadw.

Pembroke (SM 982016): Dyfed. Built in twelfth century, with outer bailey built in thirteenth century, as well as well-preserved curtain walls and round wall towers. The circular keep is an impressive feature with commanding views. Telephone: 01646 681510.

Raglan (SO 415083): Gwent, 16km (10 miles) south-west of Monmouth. Built between 1461 and 1469 on site of earlier motte and bailey. Curtain walls and hexagonal keep with commanding views. Remains of domestic and military buildings. Cadw.

Rhuddlan (SJ 026777): Clwyd, 4.8km (3 miles) south-east of Rhyl. Built between 1277 and 1278 with two gatehouses and two round corner towers. Curtain walls with square towers and moat. Cadw.

Skenfrith (SO 457202): Powys, 17.7km (11 miles) south-west of Ross-on-Wye. Dating from thirteenth century it was progressively added to during the century. Protected at one time by a moat the wall towers are 'D-plan'. The curtain walls have rounded towers, but the gatehouse is destroyed. Cadw.

Tretower (SO 182414): Powys, 17.7km (11 miles) south-east of Brecon. Built in twelfth century, added to during fourteenth and fifteenth centuries. The shell keep contains hall and chamber and the keep dates from thirteenth century. Parts of it are now a working farm. Cadw.

White Castle (SO 380168): Gwent, 8km (5 miles) east of Abergavenny. Built in the twelfth century, it was greatly remodelled in the thirteenth. Low motte with crescent bailey with curtain walls mounting towers of 'D-plan'. Small square keep with gatehouse on opposite side of motte. Cadw.

CONTACT DETAILS

Cadw can be contacted by writing to the Marketing Desk at: Cadw, Welsh Historic Monuments, Crown Building, Cathays Park, Cardiff CF10 3NQ

Telephone: 029 2050 0200; Web site: www.cadw.wales.gov.uk

Carew castle is owned and administered by Pembrokeshire Coast National Park Authority. Telephone: 01646 651782.

Manorbier castle is in private ownership but open to the public. For details of opening hours, telephone: 01834 871394.

Pembroke Medieval Walled Town and Castle. For details of opening hours and special events, telephone: 01646 683092 or 01646 681510.

Picton castle is owned and administered by the Picton Castle Trust. Telephone: 01437 751326.

It is also well worth visiting The Owain Glyn Dwr Centre, Heol Maengwyn, Machynlleth, Powys, SY20 8EE. Telephone: 01654 702827. The site of the Parliament House with full display of Glyn Dwr's life and times including details of his Great Rebellion.

There are many other sites to be found around the country of Wales and these can be identified through visiting the local Tourist Information Centres.

BIBLIOGRAPHY

Black, Jeremy, *A New History of Wales* (Stroud) 2000.

Brown, R. Allen, *Castles from the Air* (Cambridge) 1989.

Carr, A.D., *Medieval Wales* (Basingstoke) 1995.

Davies, John, *A History of Wales* (London) 1993.

Davies, R.R., *The Revolt of Owain Glyn Dwr* (Oxford) 1995.

Davis, Paul, *A Company of Forts* (Ceredigion) 2000.

Davison, Brian. K., *Castles* (London) 1986.

Forde-Johnston, James, *Great Medieval Castles of Britain* (London) 1979.

Hewitt, John, *Ancient Armour and Weapons* (London) 1996.

Ivinson, Stuart, *Anglo-Welsh Wars 1050–1300* (Wrexham) 2001.

Kinross, John, *Discovering Castles* (Aylesbury) 1973.

Morgan, Kenneth O. (ed.), *The Oxford Illustrated History of Britain* (Oxford) 1984.

Morris, John E., *The Welsh Wars of Edward I* (Facsimile reprint; Ceredigion) 1994.

Muir, Robert, *Castles and Strongholds* (London) 1990.

Salter, Mike, *The Castles of South-West Wales* (Malvern) 1994.

Tywysogion, Brut y, *The Chronicle of the Princes*.

Warner, Philip, *Sieges of the Middle Ages* (London) 1968.

I would also like to acknowledge my debt to Cadw Guide Books: Laugharne, Carreg Cennen, Raglan, *et al.*

INDEX

Page references in bold refer to illustrations

If you are interested in purchasing
other books published by Tempus, or in case you have
difficulty finding any Tempus books in your local bookshop,
you can also place orders directly through our website

www.tempus-publishing.com